CO-ATF-288

915.61 Mei
Meinardus.
St. Paul in Ephesus and the cities
 of Galatia and Cyprus.

The Lorette Wilmot Library
Nazareth College of Rochester

By the same author

The Copts in Jerusalem, Cairo, 1960

Monks and Monasteries of the Egyptian Deserts, Cairo 1960

Atlas of Christian Sites in Egypt, Cairo, 1962

Holy Land Pilgrimage, Cairo, 1962

In the Steps of the Holy Family from Bethlehem to Upper Egypt, Cairo, 1963

The Significance of Sinai, Beirut, 1963

Christian Egypt Ancient and Modern, Cairo, 1965

Cradles of Faith, Cairo, 1966

Factors in Religious Dialogue in the Middle East, Istanbul, 1968

Christian Egypt Faith and Life, Cairo, 1970

The Saints of Greece, Athens, 1970

St. Paul in Greece, Athens, 1972

St. John of Patmos and the Seven Churches of the Apocalypse, 1974

In the Footsteps of the Saints

ST. PAUL IN EPHESUS

and the Cities of Galatia and Cyprus

Otto F. A. Meinardus

CARATZAS BROTHERS, PUBLISHERS
New Rochelle, New York — 1979

LORETTE WILMOT LIBRARY
NAZARETH COLLEGE

Copyright © Lycabettus Press

All rights reserved.
Except for use in review, the reproduction or
utilization of this work in any form is
forbidden without the written permission of
the publisher.

First published in Greece by

Lycabettus Press
P.O. Box 3391
Kolonaki
Athens
Greece

Published in North America by

CARATZAS BROTHERS, PUBLISHERS
246 Pelham Road, New Rochelle,
New York 10805

ISBN: 0-89241-071-X (hardcover)
ISBN: 0-89241-044-2 (paperback)
Library of Congress Catalog
Card Number 78-51246

CONTENTS

INTRODUCTION

One hundred years ago no one thought that the ruins of Ephesus would become one of the most attractive tourist sites in the Mediterranean. Since the Middle Ages pilgrims have stopped in Ephesus to see the remains of the famous city of Diana-Artemis, and to walk in the steps of the Holy Apostles, Sts. Paul, John, and Timothy, but it was not until the second half of the 19th century, when systematic archaeological work on the site was begun, that Ephesus aroused the interest and curiosity of the European and American tourist. The first excavations were conducted by J.T. Wood on behalf of the trustees of the British Museum between 1863 and 1874. News of his discovery of the ancient site of the Artemision, one of the Seven Wonders of the Ancient World, spread rapidly, and travelers began to arrive in Smyrna (modern Izmir) and Scala Nuova (modern Kuşadasi) on their way to visit Ephesus with its wealth of antiquities. Mr. Wood, commenting on the 19th century tourists to Ephesus, made this interesting remark:

> I have seen there, perhaps, more of our American cousins than of any other nationality. I was particularly fortunate in meeting with many Americans, ladies as well as gentlemen, who caused me to form a very high estimate of the American character. I found them generally anxious to make something more than a superficial survey of the ruins, and I do not now remember any party of Americans preferring to sit down to eat and drink to making a careful examination of all the interesting objects they had come to see.

Today Ephesus is famous for a number of reasons. It is important to classicists and historians as one of the ancient cities of Ionia and as the capital of the Roman province of Asia. To students of the Bible the city is important because of its connections with St. Paul's ministry, while others relate it to the Virgin Mary's last days.

With the increasing number of visitors traveling in Asia Minor and Cyprus, either in groups or alone, the need for a commentary on the travels of the Apostle Paul in this part of the world has become apparent, especially since there exists no readily available literature to assist the Bible student in his explorations. In the early 1930's, H.V. Morton wrote *In the Steps of St. Paul,* an exciting account of his travels through Palestine, Syria, Cyprus, Turkey, and Greece, which soon became the most widely read book on the subject. But almost forty years have passed since Morton wrote, and many significant political, social, cultural, and archaeological changes have taken place in the meantime. Although some of the places and conditions he described have remained much as they were when he visited them, there have been many rapid socio-economic changes in the intervening forty years. Archaeologists have also contributed new knowledge to our previous understanding of the historic sites of Asia Minor and Cyprus. For example, Morton, agreeing with Sir William Ramsay, identified the Biblical city of Derbe with a huge mound called Gudelisin, a theory which has subsequently been disproved by M. Ballance, who has instead located Derbe at Kerti Hüyük. Turkish archaeologists have carried out excavations at the Biblical city of Perga, Canadian archaeologists have worked at Laodicea, and a team of Austrians have discovered many new sites and objects in and around Ephesus.

The question of St. Paul's identity is inevitably raised by traveling in his footsteps and reading his letters as well as the reports about him. What kind of a person was this Paul, who, guided by the Holy Spirit, took it upon himself to travel all over the Roman world to deliver the message of the crucified and risen Christ? Although we do not know the exact date of his birth, we may assume that he was born around the beginning of the Christian era in Tarsus, one of the principal cities of the Roman province of Cilicia, in southern Asia Minor. Firstly, his birth as a free citizen in a Roman province made him a Roman citizen (Acts 22:28). He had, unquestionably, in addition to his name Paul, another Roman name which, however, has remained unrecorded. Secondly, he held full rights as a citizen of his native city, of which he was proud (Acts 21:39). Thirdly, he was "a Hebrew, born of Hebrews" to strict Jewish parents. His Jewish name, Saul, had been bestowed upon him in memory of the first king of the Jewish nation. He was a Jew as much as he was a Tarsian and a Roman, and this three-fold identity has helped make him such a controversial person. To the Hebrews in the Diaspora he emphasized his Jewish origin and character; with the Greeks he conversed in their native tongue; with the Roman authorities he stressed his claims as a Roman citizen.

His physical appearance is unknown to us, except for a brief description in the apocryphal Acts of Paul and Thecla, according to which he was "a man small in size, bald-headed, bandy-legged, well-built, with eyebrows meeting, rather long nosed, and full of grace, for sometimes he seems like a man, and sometimes he has the countenance of an angel." One of the earliest iconographic representations of him appears on the 4th century sarcophagus of the Roman consul Junius Bassus, now in the crypt of St. Peter's in Rome. This relief shows the Apostle being led to his death by soldiers, his hands tied behind his back. He has a long face with a high forehead and a thick beard, and he is wearing a tunic, a knee-length undergarment, over which he has a *pallium,* or cloak. Although not included among the Twelve Disciples, St. Paul replaced St. Matthias, and by the 6th century his right to be represented in religious iconography as one of the Twelve was undisputed. Byzantine art usually showed him looking to his right, holding his letters in both hands. His tunic is either dark green or dark blue, while the *pallium,* which he wears open, is dark red.

In spite of his charismatic ministry among the peoples of Syria, Cyprus, Asia Minor, and Greece, St. Paul never became the object of a separate Christian cult. In all the principal centers of his missionary work it was one of his disciples or even another Christian saint altogether who came to be venerated. Thus, for example, the Antiochenes considered St. Peter their patron, the Cypriots, St. Barnabas, while in Iconium St. Thecla was held in the highest esteem. The same was true of St. John in Ephesus, St. Titus in Crete, St. Silas in Rhodes, and St. Dionysius the Areopagite in Athens. The lack of a specifically Pauline cult in the Eastern Mediterranean can be attributed to the clear message the Apostle preached of the crucified and risen Christ. This was in sharp contrast to the popular religion of the people he addressed, and discouraged the growth of a cult around the Apostle which otherwise easily could have developed. Moreover, St. Paul did not provide the people of the Eastern Mediterranean with any tangible cult objects for their veneration. Instead he simply preached a message, establishing a living and dynamic faith, and left the growth of the new communities to the power of the Holy Spirit.

Throughout the text I have employed the ancient names of the cities, towns, and provinces. For example, Antioch-on-the-Orontes is Antakya, the southernmost Turkish city; while Iconium, also known as Claudiconium, became known as Konya after the Arab expansion in the 7th century A.D. Yalvaç is the name of the modern village near the ruins of ancient Pisidian Antioch. After its decline, Ephesus was renamed Haghios Theologos, after St. John the Theologian who was believed to be buried there. Part of this name survived in Ayasoluk, the first Turkish name for the city. During the second half of the 14th century the Italians, who had obtained commercial concessions in the town from the Byzantines, called it Altoluogo. In 1914 the name was changed to Selçuk. After the Turkish War of Independence the town was officially named Akinçilar, although for all practical purposes Selçuk is still used.

On the thorny issue of the location of the Biblical Galatia, I have adopted the so-called "South Galatian Theory," which maintains that the Apostle wrote his Letter to the Galatians to the people of Pisidian Antioch, Iconium, Lystra, and Derbe, all cities where he had established Christian congregations on his first missionary journey. It seems to me that those who argue that this letter was addressed to the Galatians in north-central

Asia Minor around such cities as Ancyra, Tavium, and Pessinus, through which the Apostle hurried on his second missionary journey, create unnecessary problems. For if St. Paul could refer to the Christians in Philippi, Thessalonica, and Veria as "Macedonians," why should he not speak of those in Pisidian Antioch, Iconium, Lystra, and Derbe as "Galatians?" Since the death of Amyntus in 25 B.C. these towns were a part of Galatia. Following R.H. Lightfoot and Günther Bornkamm, I have assigned the composition of the Letter to the Galatians to the period of the Apostle's stay in Ephesus.

There is no unanimity of opinion among New Testament scholars about the date and place of writing of the Pauline prison letters, which are not in themselves explicit about where they were written, except that the writer is in prison. St. Paul was often held in prison. According to II Cor. 11:23, he had known "far more imprisonments, with countless beatings, and often near death." According to the Acts of the Apostles, St. Paul was only imprisoned once before he wrote to the Corinthians, namely his brief imprisonment in Philippi (Acts 16:22-40), but some scholars maintain that the prison correspondence was written from Rome. It is my belief, however, that St. Paul wrote all of these letters during his imprisonment in Ephesus which, although ignored by St. Luke, is repeatedly implied by his own testimony.

Here, as in my earlier *St. Paul in Greece,* I have relied mainly on two Biblical sources: first, the letters of the Apostle to the churches in Greece and Asia Minor, all of which I consider to be genuinely Pauline, including the circular letter to the Churches of Asia, traditionally known as the Letter to the Ephesians; and second, the Acts of the Apostles, in which St. Luke describes the missionary journeys and efforts of St. Paul and his colleagues. In addition I have referred occasionally to the Western Text of the Acts of the Apostles and to material from the New Testament Apocrypha, namely the 2nd century Acts of Paul and Thecla, and the 5th century Acts of Barnabas. The Scripture quotations in this publication are from the Revised Standard Version of the Bible, copyrighted 1946 and 1952 by the Division of Christian Education of the National Council of Churches of Christ in the U.S.A. and are used by permission.

The following pages are addressed to the religiously oriented visitor to Ephesus, southern Asia Minor, and Cyprus who is eager to explore the cities and the countryside where St. Paul journeyed, and to understand something of their history. Traveling in the footsteps of the Apostle through the former provinces of Syria, Cyprus, Cilicia, Lycaonia, Galatia, Pamphylia, and Asia still requires something of an adventurous spirit, especially if one is restricted to public transport and walking.

In my travels through the Turkish countryside, on every conceivable indigenous transport — buses and minibuses, as well as dolmushes and tractors — I was fortunate to be accompanied by my sixteen year old son, Ronald. He shared many of his instructive ideas with me, and his interest and enthusiasm were a genuine source of inspiration. I am grateful for the many helpful suggestions made by my colleagues of the American School of Classical Studies in Athens, and I would also like to thank my secretary, Mrs Sophia Hanazoglu, for preparing the manuscript for the press.

Otto F.A. Meinardus

St. Andrew's American Church
Athens, Greece, 1973

SUGGESTED CHRONOLOGY

St. Paul made three missionary journeys and a final journey to Rome. The first missionary journey was to Cyprus and Asia Minor. The second and third missionary journeys were to Asia Minor and Greece. The fourth and final journey was from Palestine to Rome.

45	St. Paul's ministry in Antioch-on-the-Orontes.
Summer of 46	Beginning of first missionary journey to Cyprus and the cities of Galatia.
Autumn of 46	Arrival in Perga.
Autumn of 47	Return from Attalia to Antioch-on-the-Orontes.
Summer of 48	The Jerusalem Conference.
Autumn of 48	Beginning of second missionary journey, from Antioch-on-the-Orontes to Derbe, Lystra, Iconium, Phrygia, and Troy.
Spring of 49	Neapolis (Kavalla), Philippi, Thessalonica, Veria, and Athens.
Spring of 50	Arrival in Corinth.
Summer of 51	Accusation before Gallio, the proconsul in Corinth.
Autumn of 51	Departure from Corinth. Return to Antioch-on-the-Orontes via Ephesus, Caesarea, and Jerusalem.
Spring of 53	Beginning of third missionary journey. Visits in Phrygia and Galatia.
Autumn of 54	Journey to Ephesus where he stayed for approximately two and one half years, during which he made a brief visit to Corinth.
Summer of 57	Macedonia.
Winter 57- 58	Corinth, for three months.
Spring of 58	Return through Macedonia to Caesarea.
Autumn of 61	Crete.

ST. PAUL'S JOURNEY TO CYPRUS AND GALATIA

St. Paul Is Commissioned In Antioch

The story of the expansion of the Christian faith in the Gentile world begins with chapter 13 of St. Luke's Acts of the Apostles. Here St. Paul takes his place as the principal character, and the scope of the narrative is broadened to include the Apostle's travels to spread the message of the Gospel among the Gentiles.

> Now in the church at Antioch there were prophets and teachers, Barnabas, Symeon who was called Niger, Lucius of Cyrene, Manaen a member of the court of Herod the tetrarch, and Saul. While they were worshiping the Lord and fasting, the Holy Spirit said, "Set apart for me Barnabas and Saul for the work to which I have called them." Then after fasting and praying they laid their hands on them and sent them off. So, being sent out by the Holy Spirit, they went down to Seleucia; and from there they sailed to Cyprus.
>
> Acts 13:1-4

These events took place in the spring of 46 A.D. in Antioch-on-the-Orontes in Syria, a city which sometimes boasted that it was the third largest city in the world. Perhaps no other city in the Eastern Mediterranean world of that time was so full of contrasts as Antioch. Just outside the city the groves of Daphne had created the legend of "Daphinici mores" which Juvenal, the 1st century Roman satirist and poet, held responsible for the

The Roman Provinces of the Eastern Mediterranean

disintegration of Roman morality when "the waters of the Syrian Orontes flowed into the Tiber." Centuries later, the English historian, Edward Gibbon, described the moral climate of Antioch,

> with its fountains and groves of bay trees, its bright buildings, its crowds of licentious votaries, its statue of Apollo, where, under the climate of Syria and the wealthy patronage of Rome, all that was beautiful in nature and in art created a sanctuary for a perpetual festival of vice.

But it was also in Antioch that the followers of Jesus Christ were first called "Christians" (Acts 11:25, 26), a name which probably originated with the Antiochene Gentiles. In the same way as the partisans of Marius, Pompey, and Herod were called Marians, Pompeians, and Herodians respectively (Matt. 23:16; Mark 3:6), so the disciples of Christ came to be known as Christians, a term which embraced all their previous designations — brethren, believers, saints, witnesses, stewards, and those of the Way.

Coming from Tarsus, Barnabas and Saul spent a full year in Antioch were "they met with the church, and taught a large company of people" (Acts 11:26). With the increasing number of Gentile converts, the church in Antioch began to shake off its Jewish characteristics and soon became the center of Gentile Christianity. Its leaders, in addition to Barnabas and Paul, were Symeon, Lucius, and Manaen. Symeon's surname Niger, or "black," suggests that he came from Africa and it is possible that he was the Simon of Cyrene who carried Jesus' cross (Mark 15:21). Lucius of Cyrene may have been the kinsman of St. Paul who added his greetings to the Christians in Ephesus (Rom. 16:21). Manaen or Menahem is spoken of as the foster-brother of Herod Antipas, tetrarch of Galilee. During a religious service the Holy Spirit instructed these Christians to send Paul and Barnabas out of Antioch to work for the Lord. The final consecration and commissioning occurred on another occasion when, after fasting and praying, their Christian brethren "laid their hands on them and sent them off."

7

Antakya: The River God Orontes, 1st century A.D., Hatay
Museum, No. 8498

Significant archaeological remains of this once so important cultural center are to be found in the Hatay Museum of Antakya, the Turkish name for Antioch-on-the-Orontes, where some fine mosaics are exhibited. Near the foot of the mountain to the north of Antakya is St. Peter's grotto, said to have been the meeting place of the Christians of Antioch. Here Barnabas and Saul may have been commissioned for their missionary work among the Gentiles. The facade of the cave, which has recently been restored, dates from the time of the Crusaders. Inside the cave are traces of a mosaic. The small recess leading to a tunnel was probably an escape route. Occasional Divine Services are celebrated here by the Catholic priest from Tarsus. The relief of a bust some 300 feet above the grotto may either be of Antigonas, Alexander the Great's companion, or Seleucus I Nicator.

A local tradition is still circulated among the Turks of Antakya according to which St. Paul stayed in a house which was later converted into the Habib Naccar Mosque at the

Antakya: Cave Church of St. Peter

4

corner of Kurtulus Caddesi and Kemal Pasha Caddesi.

The Apostle and Barnabas probably left Antioch by sailing down the Orontes River to Seleucia of Pieria, where they embarked on their sea voyage to Cyprus. The 5th century apocryphal Acts of Barnabas mentions that the Apostles had to wait three days before they could find a ship to take them to Cyprus. The memory of St. Paul's departure remained in Seleucia for many centuries. In the 19th century the piers of the outer harbor, which could be seen under water, were called after the two Apostles, the south pier after St. Paul, and the north pier after St. Barnabas.

Antakya: Altar in the Cave Church of St. Peter

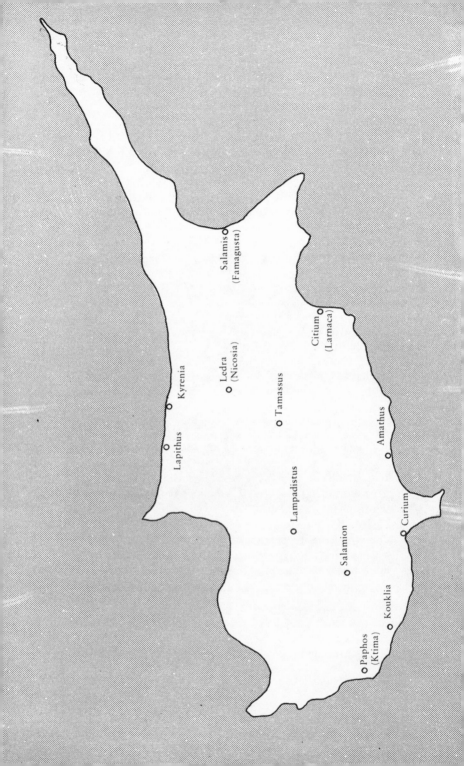

Salamis

> When they arrived at Salamis, they proclaimed the word of God in the synagogues of the Jews. And they had John to assist them.
>
> Acts 13:5

The sea journey from Seleucia to Cyprus probably took only a few hours. As they stepped ashore in the city of Salamis, Paul, Barnabas, and John Mark, Barnabas's cousin, may well have been welcomed by some of their fellow believers. St. Luke informs us that Barnabas, originally named Joseph, was born in Cyprus (Acts 4:36). The Jewish community in Salamis was large, engaging mostly in commerce, exporting Cypriot fruit, wine, flax, and honey all over the ancient Roman world. Some years earlier a number of them had been converted to Christianity when, after the martyrdom of St. Stephen in 36 A.D., some of the believers

> traveled as far as Phoenicia and Cyprus and Antioch, speaking the word to none except Jews. But there were some of them, men of Cyprus and Cyrene, who on coming to Antioch spoke to the Greeks also, preaching the Lord Jesus.
>
> Acts 11:19b

It is likely, therefore, that there was a small group of Christians in the great commercial center of Salamis. One of these converts is known to us by name, "Mnason of Cyprus, an early disciple" (Acts 21:16).

When the Romans conquered Cyprus in 58 B.C. they divided the island into four districts: Paphos, Salamis, Amathus, Lapithus. They transferred the seat of government from Salamis to New Paphos and built their main naval base and dockyards at

Cyprus: Traditional Sites Visited by St. Paul

Lapithus, now a picturesque village nine miles west of Kyrenia. Although no longer the capital, Salamis remained an important center, well known for its impressive public buildings. The harbor was one of the most important in the eastern Mediterranean, but nothing of it is visible today except some architectural remains which may be seen at low tide. After the missionaries had disembarked, they must have passed the Augustan gymnasium, which had been built not long before on the foundations of a Hellenistic one. A Roman theater which could seat 20,000 people was built one hundred years after the Apostle's visit to the city, probably on the site of a Hellenistic theater. In the palaistra the missionaries would have seen marble statues of pagan gods, many of which survived well into the Christian period despite the systematic obliteration of pagan symbols. Some statues of Zeus, Asklepios, Apollo, and Nemesis were tolerated, although after mutilation, while statues of other gods were not. Many of the discarded statues were thrown into unused rooms. Salamis experienced the fate of which Ernest Renan wrote, "O chaste and lovely forms, true gods and goddesses, tremble! The iconoclast is here. The doom has been uttered: 'You are idols!' "

Late in the first and early in the second century A.D., Roman rule in the eastern Mediterranean was challenged by Jewish revolt. The Jews of Salamis revolted with their coreligionists but were bloodily suppressed by the emperor Hadrian (117-138 A.D.) who landed on the island with an army. The Jews were expelled from Cyprus and prohibited from returning. According to rabbinical tradition, the Jewish insurrection in Salamis was preceded by a massacre of the Jews so extensive that "the sea that broke upon the shores of Cyprus was tinged with the red hue of carnage."

Although the excavations at Salamis have been extensive, no traces of any of the synagogues where the Apostles proclaimed the Word of God have been discovered. The 5th century apocryphal Acts of Barnabas says that "the synagogue was near

Salamis: Aerial View

the place called Biblia, where Barnabas, having unrolled the gospel which he had received from Matthew his fellow-labourer, began to teach the Jews." It is probable that the synagogues were near the sea. Josephus, the 1st century A.D. Jewish historian, wrote of the decision by the people of Halicarnassus in western Asia Minor to "suffer the Jews to observe their laws and sabbaths and build synagogues, as was their custom, by the sea." Most of the few synagogues which have been excavated, namely those of Delos and Aegina in Greece, Priene and Miletus in Turkey, and Stobi in Yugoslavia, were either close to the sea or near a river. The canons prescribed, after the famous prayer of Solomon upon the dedication of the Temple in Jerusalem (I Kings 8:44, Daniel 6:10, 11), that synagogues should face toward Jerusalem. Details of the content of the Apostles' message in the Cyprus synagogues have remained unrecorded, beyond the brief statement that they proclaimed the Word of God, namely the Christ.

The Cypriots consider St. Barnabas, rather than St. Paul, as their patron saint and the founder of the Christian church on their island. Barnabas was probably one of the most prominent members of the early Church before St. Paul assumed the leadership. Originally named Joseph, he may have been given the name Barnabas to indicate his role as a prophet or teacher, if we accept the traditional derivation of his name from *barnebhuah*, "son of prophecy" (Acts 4:36).

In the Church of England, Barnabas is honored with his own feast day. Although he was born in Cyprus, Barnabas must also have had family connections in Jerusalem, for John Mark was his cousin. It was in Jerusalem, morever, where he donated the proceeds from the sale of his land to the Apostles (Acts 4:37). His importance in the early Christian community can be seen in the decision of the Jerusalem church to send him to Antioch to inspect the growing church there (Acts 11:22). Before long Barnabas asked his friend Paul to come help him in Antioch. It is almost certain that it was Barnabas's influence which first led St. Paul to Cyprus.

Some years later, before embarking on his second missionary journey, St. Paul disagreed with St. Barnabas about whether

John Mark should again accompany them. Paul opposed the idea, since on the first journey John Mark had left them at Pamphylia. The three Apostles separated, Barnabas and John Mark returning to Cyprus, while St. Paul went on to travel with Silas and Timothy through Cilicia, Galatia, Macedonia, and Achaia.

> After some days Paul said to Barnabas, "Come let us return and visit the brethren in every city where we proclaimed the word of the Lord, and see how they are." And Barnabas wanted to take with them John called Mark. But Paul thought best not to take with them one who had withdrawn from them in Pamphylia, and had not gone with them to the work. And there arose a sharp contention, so that they separated from each other; Barnabas took Mark with him and sailed away to Cyprus."
>
> Acts 15:36-39

There is no scriptural record to tell us what happened to Barnabas and Mark after their return to Cyprus, but according to tradition, they continued their missionary work and Barnabas became the first Bishop of Salamis, his native city, where he is said to have been martyred and secretly buried by his cousin Mark. His brother Aristobulus, so the Cypriots say, was the first missionary to Britain. St. Paul later mentioned those "who belong to the family of Aristobulus" (Rom. 16:10), but this was a very common name, and it is doubtful that the name refers to the same person. According to a medieval legend, St. Barnabas, after becoming bishop of Salamis, was supposed to have been sent to Italy by St. Peter, where he converted St. Clement in Rome and later became Bishop of Milan.

The ruins of ancient Salamis are about six miles north of Famagusta on the road to Trikomo and Kantara. The entrance to the site is on the east side of the road. Opposite the entrance another road leads to the Monastery of St. Barnabas, one mile west of Salamis. In 478 A.D. Anthemios, Archbishop of Constantia (Salamis) had a vision telling him where St. Barnabas was buried. When the site was searched the saint's relics were found together with a copy of the Gospel of St. Matthew in St. Barnabas's handwriting. The Gospel was then presented to the emperor Zeno (474-491 A.D.) in Constantinople, who conferred imperial privileges on Archbishop Anthemios. Thereafter the Archbishop of Cyprus could sign his name in red ink, wear the imperial purple, and carry the imperial scepter. The discovery of the relics helped end the controversy between Cyprus and Antioch-on-the-Orontes. Cyprus had been administered by the diocese of the Orient in Antioch until it was made independent by the Third Ecumenical Council in Ephesus in 431 A.D., a decision disputed by Antioch. The story of the discovery of the relics is portrayed in four life-size wall paintings in the monastery church of St. Barnabas. They were painted by the three monks who are also brothers, Barnabas, Chariton, and Stephanos, in charge of the monastery.

Halfway between the forest of Salamis and the monastery is a megalithic monument said to have been the prison of St. Catherine, the Alexandrian virgin martyr. Excavations here brought to light various vases and the skeletons of two horses harnassed together, with iron bits still in their teeth. Throughout the Middle Ages, pilgrims on their way to the Holy Land stopped in Salamis to visit this monument. In 1542 the Swiss pilgrim Jodicus de Meggen described the monument as the "tomb of St. Catherine." In 1566 Christoph Führer wrote of the subterranean "prison of St. Catherine" which seemed to be cut out of the rock. On the feast of St. Catherine, November 25, people from the neighboring villages attend services conducted here.

Paphos

When they had gone through the whole island as far as Paphos ...

Acts 13:6a

The phrase "whole island" may have been intended to convey

the idea that the Apostles made a tour of the Jewish communities on the island, preaching in each synagogue. The Acts of Barnabas states that they visited Lapithus, nine miles west of Kyrenia. Here they were not well received because "an idol festival was celebrated in the theater," so they traveled on "through the mountains and came to the city of Lampadistus." This place should be identified with the famous resort of Kalopanayiotis, forty-six miles southwest of Nicosia in the Marathassa Valley. In their wanderings they are also said to have taken refuge in "the village of the Ledrians," because some Jews who opposed them were searching for them. Ledra is the ancient name for Nicosia, the present capital of Cyprus. The Greeks call it Lefkosia and the Turks Lefkosha.

It is impossible to reconstruct the route the Apostles took in the journey across the island, and the many local traditions cannot really be considered as historical testimonies. One of these legends tells that the missionaries traveled to Citium, the Chittim of the Old Testament, known today as Larnaca, and then proceeded inland to the rich copper mines of Tamassus. In Citium St. Paul is said to have converted Heracleides who, on the return of St. Barnabas to the island after he had left St. Paul at the start of his second missionary journey, was consecrated bishop of Tamassus. The skull of this early Cypriot convert still reposes in the Convent of St. Heracleides in the village of Politiko, thirteen miles southwest of Nicosia. If the Apostles passed through Citium, they might have been preceded by Lazarus, the brother of Mary and Martha, who is believed to have come over to Cyprus after being raised at Bethany. The Cypriots believe that Lazarus was the first bishop of Citum and that he died there. His tomb is still shown beneath the Church of St. Lazarus, though the body was stolen and is claimed to be in the Cathedral of Marseilles. Recently it was reported that partial remains of St. Lazarus were found wrapped in strips of bark in a sarcophagus under the altar of the church.

It is believed that the missionaries, before reaching Paphos, stopped for rest in the village of Salamion, eighteen miles to the northeast. Below the 16th century Church of the Panagia Elëousa in Salamion is a field where Paul and Barnabas are said to have

13

rested and eaten at midday. The olive pits they discarded became the trees which are still there today. Another story, recorded in the Acts of Barnabas, relates that during their journey through the island the Apostles came to the Temple of Apollo Hylates at Curium, ten miles west of Limassol, where they saw a group of young men and women stripped naked for a race. Considerably shocked by the sight, they turned back and took another road. Today Curium is famous for its Roman theater, discovered by archaeologists from the University of Pennsylvania. Shakespearian plays are performed here annually.

From Curium the missionaries went on to Old Paphos, now occupied by the village of Kouklia eleven miles east of modern Paphos. Aphrodite, goddess of love and fertility, was born near ancient Paphos of the sperm of Zeus which had been washed up on the shore, and a temple was dedicated to her in the city. Even today during the winter months great masses of white foam are cast up on the beach near the ruins of the temple. In a collection of stories compiled in the 16th century by Tommaso Porcacchi of Castiglione, Old Paphos was described as a place where "naked men and women sacrificed to Venus (Aphrodite), but at the prayer of St. Barnabas, a native of Cyprus, the temple fell and the scandal ceased." Iohann van Kootwyck visited the island in 1599 and heard the same account, with the addition that after the destruction of the Temple of Aphrodite, the Apostles consecrated Epaphras bishop of the town.

If the missionaries ever went to the Temple of Aphrodite, from it they would have moved along the coastal road to New Paphos, the administrative capital of the island during the Roman occupation.

They came upon a certain magician, a Jewish false prophet, named Bar-Jesus. He was with the proconsul, Sergius Paulus, a man of intelligence, who summoned Barnabas and Saul and sought to hear the word of God. But Elymas the magician (for that is the meaning of his name) withstood them, seeking to turn away the proconsul from the faith. But Saul, who is also called Paul, filled with the Holy Spirit, looked intently at him and said, "You son of the devil, you enemy of all righteousness, full of all deceit and villainy, will you not stop making crooked the straight paths of the Lord? And now, behold, the hand of the Lord is upon you, and you shall be blind and unable to see the sun for a time." Immediately mist and darkness fell upon him and he went about seeking people to lead him by the hand. Then the proconsul believed, when he saw what had occurred, for he was astonished at the teaching of the Lord.

Acts 13:6b-12

Augustus had divided the provinces of the Roman Empire in two classes. The more peaceable districts, where no troops were required to preserve order, were administered by the senate and ruled by a proconsul, who had lictors with fasces, or rods for scourging, but no military power. The more troublesome provinces were kept under the personal administration of the emperor. They were ruled by a propraetor or legate, who in turn employed procurators for each district. In the days of Our Lord, Syria was administered by a legate (Luke 2:2) and Judaea by a procurator. Although Cyprus had once been included in the imperial province of Cilicia, the island was declared a senatorial province in 22 B.C. St. Luke is therefore right in calling the governor of Cyprus a proconsul, a man responsible to the senate and the people rather than to the emperor.

The proconsul's name was Sergius Paulus, but we know little of him except that he had an inquiring mind. He both employed a magician and summoned the Apostles to him as soon as they arrived in the capital. The employment of a magician by the proconsul was not unusual at that time. The famous Roman general Marius (155-86 B.C.) engaged a Jewish prophetess upon whom he relied in his campaigns, Pompey and Caesar sought information from oriental astrology, and Brutus, at the beginning of the Republic, consulted the Delphic oracle. Tacitus, the great Latin historian, well aware of the widespread employment of astrologers and sorcerers, referred to them as a class of men who "will always be discarded and always be cherished" (Hist. i, 22).

The encounter of St. Paul with Bar-Jesus has often been seen as a mere copy of St. Peter's dealings with Simon Magus (Acts 8:9-24), but Bar-Jesus had committed a very different offense from that of Simon who, far from opposing St. Peter, professed conversion. In contrast, Bar-Jesus appeared as a Jewish rival who tried to prevent the proconsul from hearing the Christian message. St. Paul met Bar-Jesus on his own terms. Filled with the Holy Spirit, he looked intently at him and cursed him so that at least temporarily he lost his eyesight. Some interpreters maintain that St. Paul denounced Bar-Jesus' spiritual blindness, which later led to the story that the Apostle had inflicted actual physical blindness upon him. St. Luke's point is that the blinding of the false prophet opened the eyes of the proconsul. Whether the conversion of Sergius Paulus had any immediate effect on the spread of Christianity in Cyprus we do not know. It is unlikely that large numbers of Cypriots would have followed the faith of their Roman administrator, particularly as proconsuls were usually only appointed for a one year period.

From this point on in the narrative St. Luke no longer refers to the Apostle as Saul but only as Paul. Both Origen and Jerome believed that Paul changed his name after his famous convert, Sergius Paulus. This is, however, most unlikely, for Paul may well have had the name all his life. The change in name at this point in Acts reflects his change in role. Earlier in Acts he was known as Saul, a Jew among Jews, but now, standing in the halls of the Roman proconsul, he speaks as a Roman citizen among Gentiles, using the name Paul.

The Christians of New Paphos maintained that Paul and Barnabas were imprisoned and scourged in the city before meeting the proconsul. During the 15th and early 16th centuries travelers were shown the prison beneath the Church of the Friars Minor as the place where the Apostles were held. The ruins of this church and the prison were still pointed out to travelers late in the 16th century. Cornelius van Bruyn, however, who visited Paphos in 1683, was told that "the prison of St. Paul was near the old castle on a hill." General Louis Palma di Casnola, who served as American consul in Cyprus from 1865 to 1873, wrote that "when St. Paul visited Paphos, he was so badly treated that he declared the citizens to be the worst men of the world." Seigneur de Villamont, who visited Baffo, as New Paphos was called by the Turks, in 1589, was told of "the bonds with which St. Paul was bound."

Near the west end of the 13th century Church of the Chrysopolitissa, enclosed by a fence, stands part of a column known

Paphos: The Traditional Column of the Flagellation of St. Paul

as the Column of the Flagellation of St. Paul. It is 1.20 m. high and has a diameter of 0.55 m. In many ways the column is similar to the flagellation columns in the Patriarchal Cathedral of St. George in Istanbul and in the Franciscan Chapel of St. Mary Magdalene in the Church of the Holy Sepulcher in Jerusalem. Tradition has it that St. Paul was tied to this column when he was scourged "forty less one" (II Cor. 11:24). The "forty less one" was not the number of strokes he received, but rather the type of whip, which had 39 cords tied in three bands of thirteen cords. In this connection the 19th century writer D.G. Hogarth records an interesting observation, according to which the imprint of St. Paul's hand appears on this column once a year, curiously enough only on St. John's day.

Pamphylia

Now Paul and his company set sail from Paphos, and came to Perga in Pamphylia. And John left them and returned to Jerusalem.

Acts 13:13

In the late summer of 46, Paul and his companions sailed from the harbor of Paphos across the Pamphylian Sea into the Bay of Attalia. The crossing may have taken them three days. The text suggests that they sailed up the Cestrus, now known as the Aksu River, to the harbor of Perga. Strabo, the 1st century B.C. geographer, informs us that the harbor was sixty stadia or seven miles upstream. The city of Perga itself, today near the village of Murtuna, was five miles west of the river. This location was ideal, for it was far enough from the coast to escape pirate attacks and yet had excellent communications. The city has been excavated by Professor Arit Müfit Mansel of the University of Istanbul.

We do not know how long Paul, Barnabas, and John Mark remained in Perga, although a tradition based upon the apoc-

18

ryphal Acts of Barnabas speaks of a two month stay. It is unlikely that they proceeded inland immediately, for here "John left them and returned to Jerusalem." There is no indication of the reason why John Mark left. Perhaps, being a kinsman of Barnabas, he was jealous of St. Paul who was rapidly assuming the leadership, or perhaps he was afraid of the brigands who haunted the Taurus Mountains. Perhaps he hesitated to embark upon a largely Gentile mission in the interior of Asia Minor, but if this were the case it would have been easier for him to have left Paul and Barnabas in Paphos and returned from there directly to Jerusalem. It is not unreasonable to think that St. Paul's plans to bring the Gospel to the Gentiles appeared blasphemous to John Mark. Whatever the cause of their separation, it shook the Apostle's faith in John Mark for many years to come (Acts 15: 36-41), although it did not affect St. Paul's feelings toward Barnabas. St. Paul and John Mark were eventually reconciled, for many years later in his Letter to the Colossians Paul wrote of "Mark the cousin of Barnabas (concerning whom you have received instructions — if he comes to you, receive him)" (Col. 4:10).

Pisidian Antioch

But they passed on from Perga and came to Antioch of Pisidia.

Acts 13:14a

The mountain passes of the Taurus were closed during the winter months, so Paul and Barnabas must have traveled inland sometime in the autumn of 46. We do not know if they walked or used the numerous horse coaches which transported people and goods along the excellent Roman roads connecting all the populated centers of Asia Minor. In passing from Perga to Pisidian Antioch, the travelers passed from the province of Pamphylia into the province of Galatia, in which they remained until

they returned to Perga. The term "Galatia" in Asia Minor derives from the Gauls, the Celtic people who invaded central Europe in the 4th and 3rd centuries B.C. Many Gauls settled on the Atlantic coast and gave their name to the country which roughly corresponds to modern France. Another group of Gauls moved into and dominated Asia Minor early in the 3rd century B.C. but in the latter part of the century they were driven by Attalus I of Pergamum out of the rich cities of the west coast into the high plateaus of the interior, where they settled down to an agricultural life. In 25 B.C. Augustus made a Roman province of the area in which they had settled, including parts of Pontus and Phrygia which became known as Pontus Galaticus and Phrygia Galatica. The southern section, Phrygia Galatica, was commercially and politically by far the more important.

Several scholars have suggested that St. Paul's decision to move inland across Pamphylia and over the rough mountain paths to the plateaus of Pisidia and Lycaonia was because of an illness he contracted on the coast of Asia Minor. Sir William M. Ramsay has suggested that malaria led him to go to the higher altitude of the interior as far as Pisidian Antioch, 3,000 feet above sea level. He certainly was suffering from some illness, the thorn in the flesh (II Cor. 12:7) as he made clear:

> You know it was because of a bodily ailment that I preached the gospel to you at first; and though my condition was a trial to you, you did not scorn or despise me, but received me as an angel of God, as Christ Jesus.
>
> Gal. 4:13, 14

Several factors could have contributed to the weakness of the Apostle. He had just traveled through most of Cyprus and the dispute with John Mark may also have sapped his strength.

The journey from Perga to the Pisidian highlands remained

The Cities of Southern Asia Minor

an unforgettable experience to which Paul later alluded in II
Corinthians when he wrote of being "in danger from rivers,
danger from robbers" (11:26). The floods of the Pisidian highlands had been mentioned by Strabo who wrote of the Cestrus
and Eurymedon rivers tumbling down the heights and precipices
to the Pamphylian Sea. The Apostle's reference to danger from
robbers was certainly justified, as W.C. Conybeare pointed out:
"No population through the midst of which St. Paul ever trav-
elled abounded more in those perils of robbers than the wild
and lawless clans of the Pisidian Highlanders." We do not know
if they traveled by way of Lake Ascania and Lake Limnai or
more directly through Adada. The ordinary rate of travel was
15 to 20 miles a day, so the journey would have taken them
approximately ten days.

Pisidian Antioch was one of sixteen Antiochs founded by
Seleucus I Nicator (312-281 B.C.), and it was made a free city

Near Side: Waterfalls of the Melas River, Manavgat, Selâlési

by the Romans in 189 B.C. By the last quarter of the 1st century B.C. the city, known officially as Caesareia Antiocheia, was a major Roman colony, one of the six colonies established by the emperor Augustus in the troublesome highlands of Pisidia and the major city in the southern part of Galatia. As a colony, its primary purpose was as a military post in which Roman veterans were given administrative duties and civil privileges. The Romans, of course, constituted the ruling class, electing their own magistrates, or duumviri. In many ways it was a detached fragment of imperial Rome. In addition to being a garrison, it was also an administrative center. The intellectual section of the population was Greek, while the majority of the population was Phrygian.

Pisidian Antioch was an important city to the Romans in their war with the Homanadenses, a people who had preyed on Pisidian Phrygia. In 12 B.C. Augustus appointed consul the capable Publius Sulpicius Quirinius, who pacified the Homanadenses and the whole Taurus range. He left no man free in the countryside and forced the younger generation to adopt Roman customs. By 6 B.C. the war was over and Publius Quirinius was transferred to Syria, of which he was governor when Jesus Christ was born in Bethlehem (Luke 2:2).

The Jewish community in Pisidian Antioch was not large for they only had one synagogue. We have one non-Biblical indication of a Jewish colony in the city. A 2nd or 3rd century A.D. epitaph refers to a Jewess of Antioch named Debora, a citizen of Antioch married to a man named Pamphylius of Apollonia. The epitaph says that "her ancestors held many honors in her fatherland."

The ruins of Pisidian Antioch are on the lower slopes of the majestic mountain known as Sultan Dagh approximately one mile northeast of the town of Yalvaç on the right bank of the Anthius River. In 1833 the Reverend Francis Vyvyan Jago Arundell, British chaplain in Smyrna, rediscovered the site and wrote,

> The remains of the aqueduct, of which twenty-one arches are perfect, are the most splendid I ever beheld....not a

church, nor any priest to officiate, where Paul and Barnabas, and their successors, converted the thousands of idolaters to the true faith.

The major Roman remains of Pisidian Antioch have since been excavated by archaeologists from the University of Michi-

Pisidian Antioch: Conjectural Reconstruction of the Temple of Augustus. Source: Robinson, D.M., *Art Bulletin* IX, 1926-27, Fig.3

gan. The Roman city had two large squares separated by a broad flight of twelve steps. The upper square was named after Augustus, the lower after Tiberius. At the top of the stairs stood three triumphal archways, and in the square of Augustus was a temple dedicated to the local fertility god named Men, whose symbol was a bull's head. Among the many inscriptions found at Pisidian Antioch was one referring to Lucius Sergius Paullus the Younger, whom Sir William M. Ramsay believed to be the son of Sergius Paulus, the proconsul of Cyprus.

And on the sabbath day they went into the synagogue and sat down. After the reading of the law and the prophets, the rulers of the synagogue sent to them, saying, "Brethren, if you have any word of exhortation for the people, say it." So Paul stood up, and motioning with his hand said:

"Men of Israel, and you that fear God, listen. The God of this people Israel chose our fathers and made the people great during their stay in the land of Egypt, and with uplifted arm he led them out of it. And for about forty years he bore with them in the wilderness. And when he had destroyed seven nations in the land of Canaan, he gave them their land as an inheritance, for about four hundred and fifty years. And after that he gave them judges until Samuel the prophet. Then they asked for a king; and God gave them Saul the son of Kish, a man of the tribe of Benjamin, for forty years. And when he had removed him he raised up David to be their king; of whom he testified and said, 'I have found in David the son of Jesse a man after my heart, who will do all my will.' Of this man's posterity God has brought to Israel a Savior, Jesus, as he promised. Before his coming John had preached a baptism of repentance to all the people of Israel. And as John was finishing his course, he said, 'What do you suppose that I am? I am not he. No, but after me one is coming, the sandals of whose feet I am not worthy to untie.'

"Brethren, sons of the family of Abraham, and those among you that fear God, to us has been sent the message of this salvation. For those who live in Jerusalem and their rulers, because they did not recognize him nor understand the utterances of the prophets which are read every Sabbath, fulfilled these by condemning him. Though they could charge him with nothing deserving death, yet they asked Pilate to have him killed. And when they had fulfilled all that was written of him, they took him down from the tree, and laid him in a tomb. But God raised him from the dead; and for many days he appeared to those who came up with him from Galilee to Jerusalem, who are now his witnesses to the people. And we bring you the good news that God promised to the fathers, this he has fulfilled to us their children by raising Jesus; as also it is written in the second psalm,

'Thou art my Son,
today I have begotten thee.'
And as for the fact that he raised him from the dead, no more to return to corruption, he spoke in this way,
'I will give you the holy and sure blessings of David.'
Therefore he says also in another psalm,
'Thou wilt not let thy Holy One see corruption.'
For David, after he had served the counsel of God in his own generation, fell asleep, and was laid with his fathers, and saw corruption; but he whom God raised up saw no corruption. Let it be known to you therefore, brethren, that through this man forgiveness of sins is proclaimed to you, and by him every one that believes is freed from everything from which you could not be freed by the law of Moses. Beware, therefore, lest there come upon you what is said in the prophets:

'Behold, you scoffers, and wonder, and perish; for I do a deed in your days,
a deed you will never believe, if one declares it to you.' "

Acts 13: 14b-41

When the Apostles entered the synagogue, wearing the tallith, the garment worn by Jews at prayer, they sat down with the rest of the congregation. After the prayers and the appointed readings they were invited to address the assembly. The example of Jesus (Luke 4:16) showed that, according to Jewish custom, a person wishing to speak in the synagogue could do so. St. Paul's sermon was inspired by Septuagint readings of the Law and the Prophets. It has been suggested that the lessons were from Deuteronomy 1:1-3:22 and Isaiah 1:1-22.

Although the speech as recorded in Acts 13:16-41 cannot be considered a verbatim transcript, there is good reason to believe that St. Luke may have followed the general outline of St. Paul's approach to the Hellenistic Jewish audience in Pisidian Antioch. His main ideas were that Jesus is the divinely promised offspring from the House of David, that although rejected by the Jews of Jerusalem, He is now presented as Savior to the Jews of the diaspora and, finally, that both His crucifixion and His resurrection were foretold in the Scriptures and offer the forgiveness of sins. As G.H.C. Macgregor said, "Paul's line of argument here is as suitable to a Hellenistic-Jewish synagogue as are his words in Athens to a highly educated Greek audience."

> As they went out, the people begged that these things might be told them the next sabbath. And when the meeting of the synagogue broke up, many Jews and devout converts to Judaism followed Paul and Barnabas, who spoke to them and urged them to continue in the grace of God.
>
> The next sabbath almost the whole city gathered together to hear the word of God. But when the Jews saw the multitudes, they were filled with jealousy, and contradicted what was spoken by Paul, and reviled him. And Paul and Barnabas spoke out boldly, saying, "It was necessary that the word of God should be spoken first to you. Since you thrust it from you, and judge yourselves unworthy of eternal life, behold, we turn to the Gentiles. For so the Lord has commanded us, saying, I have set you to be a light for the Gentiles, that you may bring salvation to the uttermost parts of the earth."
>
> Acts 13:42-47

The Reverend F.V.J. Arundell, the 19th century rediscoverer of Pisidian Antioch, remarked that "if Syrian Antioch had the privilege of being the spot where the disciples of Jesus were first denominated by the name of their master, Antioch of Pisidia stands out as prominently distinguished, as the place where the Jews, having rejected the offer of salvation, the tidings and privileges of the gospel were offered to the Gentile world."

The events in Pisidian Antioch were an important stage in the development of Christianity. For the first time a Christian church was set up independent of the Jewish community, a major step in the subsequent establishment of Gentile congregations.

> And when the Gentiles heard this, they were glad and glorified the word of God; and as many as were ordained to eternal life believed. And the word of the Lord spread throughout all the region. But the Jews incited the devout women of high standing and the leading men of the city, and stirred up persecution against Paul and Barnabas, and drove them out of their district. But they shook off the dust from their feet against them, and went to Iconium. And the disciples were filled with joy and with the Holy Spirit.
>
> Acts 13:48-52

We do not know whether or not the magistrates were involved in the persecution, but "women of high standing and the leading men of the city" clearly were. Strabo, who knew well the social position of women in the towns of Asia Minor, speaks in strong terms of the power and influence they possessed. It is possible that the Apostle was "beaten with rods" since he mentions in II Corinthians 11:25 that altogether "three times I have been beaten with rods." The stay in Pisidian Antioch may well have extended over several weeks, because the jealousy of the Jews would not have been so aroused until after the establishment of a separate Christian community.

Before they left the city, however, the Apostles followed the instructions of their Lord by shaking the dust from their feet (Mk. 6:11, Mt. 10:14) so as not to be defiled by a heathen community.

Iconium

> Now at Iconium they entered together into the Jewish synagogue, and so spoke that a great company believed, both of Jews and of Greeks. But the unbelieving Jews stirred up the Gentiles and poisoned their minds against the brethren. So they remained for a long time, speaking boldly for the Lord, who bore witness to the word of his grace, granting signs and wonders to be done by their hands. But the people of the city were divided; some sided with the Jews, and some with the apostles. When an attempt was made by both Gentiles and Jews, with their rulers, to molest them and to stone them, they learned of it and fled to Lystra and Derbe.
>
> Acts 14:1-6a

From Pisidian Antioch, the Apostles would have taken the Roman military road southeast across the mountains to Lystra and Derbe. This road was known as the Via Sebaste and was built by the propraetor Cornutus Aquila in 6 B.C. for Augustus. From Antioch this road went through Selki, where the 44th and 45th Roman milestones have been found.

Before reaching Lystra, however, they would have turned more to the east, proceeding straight to Iconium, a frontier town between Phrygia and Lycaonia. They would have covered the sixty miles in two or three days. According to Xenophon, Iconium was part of Phrygia, while Strabo referred to it as belonging to Lycaonia. In the first century A.D. Iconium, unlike Pisidian Antioch, was still a Greek city without Roman colonists, for it was not until the reign of Hadrian (117-138 A.D.) that this city became a colony. The Apostles resumed their work, this time in the synagogue of Iconium, and they seemed to have had considerable success. Again, some Jews were hostile to them, but they remained in Iconium, probably for several months. In Pisidian Antioch the Apostles were expelled by magisterial action; here in Iconium, however, it was mob violence that led to their departure.

Iconium is the scene of the delightful romance recorded in the second century apocryphal Acts of Paul and Thecla. This book was widely circulated in the early Church and Thecla became one of the most popular saints both in the Latin West and Byzantine East. The Acts of Paul and Thecla record that it was St. Paul's custom to send his disciple Titus ahead of him to any new city in order to advise the inhabitants of his arrival. A man in Iconium, Onesiphorus, waited on the Royal Road and invited St. Paul to his house where "there was great joy, and bending of knees, and breaking of bread." St. Paul began to speak about self-control, virginity, prayer, and the resurrection. While he addressed those who were "in the church in the house of Onesiphorus" Thecla, an eighteen year old girl, sat at the open window of her adjacent house and listened attentively and gladly to the words of the Apostle. Her mother, Theocleia, became seriously alarmed about the intensity and eagerness with which Thecla followed the words of St. Paul, so she turned to Thecla's fiancé, Thamyris, and said, "I have a strange story to tell thee, Thamyris; for assuredly for three days and three nights Thecla does not rise from the window, neither to eat nor to drink, she is so devoted to a foreigner teaching deceitful discourses, that I wonder how a virgin of such modesty is so hardly beset." Both Theocleia and Thamyris tried to convince Thecla to turn away from the Apostle, but the more they spoke the more she became enchanted with the voice and message of St. Paul. The Apostle was brought by Thamyris before the governor and, after witnessing to the power of Jesus Christ in front of his accusers, he was thrown into prison. When Thecla learned this, she left her mother's house at night and bribed her way into the prison where "she went in beside Paul, and, sitting at his feet, she heard the great things of God as she kissed his chains." The following day, Thamyris and his friends found Thecla in the prison cell with the Apostle. The governor ordered the Apostle to be scourged and expelled from the city. Thecla was condemned to be burned in the theater, "in order that all women that have been taught by this man might be afraid." Having made the sign of the cross, she mounted naked upon the pyre. They lighted the wood, but a miracle of water and hail quenched the fire and Thecla was saved.

St. Paul, with Onesiphorus and his family, were hiding in a new tomb outside the city where they mourned and fasted for six days believing that Thecla had perished in Iconium. Thecla, meanwhile, was searching for the Apostle when she met the son of Onesiphorus who had gone to buy bread for the fugitives, and with him she returned to the Apostle. Great was the rejoicing and Thecla said to St. Paul: "I shall cut my hair, and follow thee withersoever thou goest."

St. Paul and Thecla returned to Pisidian Antioch. As they entered the city, Alexander, an important high priest, became enamoured of Thecla and tried to purchase her from the Apostle. While Thecla found herself embraced by the pagan high priest, there occurred what Sir William M. Ramsay called "the detestable incident of Paul's denial and desertion of Thecla." "I know not the woman whom thou speakest of, nor is she mine," said St. Paul. Thecla, however, "tore his (Alexander's) cloak, and pulled off his crown, and made him a laughingstock." Angered at this humiliation, Alexander led Thecla before the governor who condemned her to the wild beasts. She was thrown naked to a fierce lioness, but the animal licked her feet and she was saved. For a second time she was stripped and thrown into the arena, and lions and bears and a fierce lioness were let loose upon her. Again Thecla was saved by the lioness which tore the bear asunder, but was in turn slain by the lion. Thecla prayed, and when she had ended her supplication she saw a great tank of water into which she lept, saying, "In the name of Jesus Christ I am baptized on my last day." A cloud formed about her so that the beasts would not touch her and her nakedness could not be seen. Although more wild beasts were let into the arena, none of them touched her. Then they bound her by the feet between the bulls and put hot irons under the animals' privy parts, but the burning flame consumed the ropes and she was freed. This was the last of her sufferings.

Her garments were brought and she put them on. The governor listened to her testimony to the living God and released her, and the people shouted, "There is one God, the God of Thecla," so that the foundations of the theater were shaken.

Tryphanea, a wealthy widow whose daughter was dead, took Thecla into her keeping and treated her as a second child. A coin with the Greek legend of King Polemon II on one side and Queen Tryphanea on the other assures us of the historicity of the wealthy widow in the story.

The romance ends with Thecla having dressed herself as a boy in search of St. Paul whom she found at Myra. Here she shared her sufferings for Christ's sake. "I have received the baptism, Paul, for He that hath worked together with thee for the Gospel hath worked in me in my baptism." Then Thecla returned to the house of Onesiphorus in Iconium where she fell weeping upon the pavement where Paul used to sit and teach her. Later, Thecla is said to have traveled to Seleucia of Isauria and to Rome to see Paul, but he had died. Shortly afterwards Thecla died, "and she is buried about two or three stadia from the tomb of her master Paul." In this beautiful early Christian romance it is impossible to separate legend from history. Yet, the message of this story provided confidence and inspiration to a Christian community in Galatia that was exposed to fierce persecution.

In the 4th century this story was written down in sub-Akhmimic, a dialect of the Coptic language spoken in Upper Egypt, and in the areas where this dialect was spoken there are several funerary chapels with crude iconographical representations of St. Paul and Thecla. The best preserved of these chapels is the 5th century Chapel of Peace in the necropolis of al-Bagawat in Kharga Oasis.

The site of ancient Iconium is now occupied by modern Konya, the chief town of the district of the same name. Except for the antiquities exhibited in the Konya Archaeological Museum, there are no visible remains of Roman Iconium in the modern city. Nearby are the twin conical hills which were known as the peaks of St. Philip and St. Thecla. From a distance, St. Philip's peak, about six miles northwest of the city, seems to stand over Konya like a guardian. According to tradition, St. Philip of Bethsaida (John 1:44) went to Hierapolis and Ephesus via Iconium, where he was held in great esteem.

Of all the Galatian cities visited by St. Paul, only Iconium obtained a lasting place in the history of the region. Towards the end of the 11th century it became the capital of the Selçuk Sultans, and it later played a significant role in the emergence of the Ottoman Empire. In 1097 the Crusaders, on their way to Jerusalem, occupied the lower city for a short time. About one hundred years later, the Crusaders under Frederick Barbarossa defeated the Selçuk Turks at Konya. The Selçuks retired to the city's citadel where they withstood the Crusaders' siege. In the 13th century the celebrated Muslim mystic Jalal ad-Din Rumi settled in Konya where he founded a dervish order whose influence spread throughout the Islamic world. The home of the

Al-Bagawat: Fifth Century Wall Painting of SS. Paul and Thecla in the Chapel of Peace

Whirling Dervishes, the Tekke of Mevlana, is now an Islamic museum, and the tomb of the order's founder is next door. The central passage from Jalal ad-Din Rumi's famous *Song of the Reed Flute* cries out in ecstasy of the love of God:

> Hail to thee, then, O Love, sweet madness!
> Thou who healest all our infirmities!
> Who art the physician of our pride and self-conceit!
> Who art our Plato and our Galen!
> Love exalts our earthly bodies to heaven,
> And makes the very hills to dance with joy!
> O lover, 'twas love that gave life to Mount Sinai,
> When it quaked, and Moses fell down in a swoon.

Lystra

> (They) fled to Lystra and Derbe, cities of Lycaonia, and to the surrounding country, and there they preached the gospel.
>
> Acts 14:6,7

Lystra was about twenty miles southwest of Iconium, and we assume that the Apostles traveled on the Via Sebaste which connected Iconium and Lystra. Today the site of Lystra is about two miles south of Karaağac on the north bank of the Kopru River, on the road from Konya to Khatyn Serai. The site was discovered in 1885 by the American archaeologist J. R. Sitlington Sterrett, who found an altar still standing in its original position. The altar stone, approximately three and a half feet high and

Konya: The Tekke of Mevlana and the Selemiye Çamii

twelve inches thick, has the following Latin inscription:

DIVUM AUG(ustum)
COL(onia) IUL(ia) FE
LIX GEMINA
LUSTRA
CONSE
CRAVIT
D(ecreto) D(ecurionum)

Gemina Lustra, the Fortunate, being a Julian colony, dedicated Augustus Caesar as a god: (the altar) being decreed by the Urban Council.

The text indicates the existence of a temple dedicated to Augustus in Lystra. This may have been the Temple of Zeus referred to in Acts 14:13 as being "in front of the city," for in Ancyra the Augusteum was outside the city.

The altar stone now stands in the courtyard of the Konya Archaeological Museum. Its catalogue number is 796. The other remains from the high and steep mound are chiefly epigraphic, although there are some traces of a Byzantine church and several large tombs. At one time the mound was fortified, but it is too small to have been more than a citadel for a larger settlement.

Although the Roman element in Lystra was small, and the city's aristocracy was Greek, Augustus had made the city a Roman colony. The people with whom the Apostles first came in contact were the uneducated local population, which spoke to them in their Lycaonian language. No archaeological remains of a synagogue have been found in Lystra, and no mention is made either of a synagogue or a Jewish community in Lystra, so we must assume that if there were Jews living in the city they probably worshipped in a *proseuche,* a temporary place of prayer, as did the Jews in Philippi.

Now at Lystra there was a man sitting, who could not use his feet; he was a cripple from birth, who had never walked. He listened to Paul speaking; and Paul, looking intently at him and seeing that he had faith to be made well, said in a loud voice, "Stand upright on your feet." And he sprang up and walked. And when the crowds saw what Paul had done, they lifted up their voices, saying in Lycaonian, "The gods have come down to us in the likeness of men!" Barnabas they called Zeus, and Paul, because he was the chief speaker, they called Hermes. And the priest of Zeus, whose temple was in front of the city, brought oxen and garlands to the gates and wanted to

Lystra: Altar Stone, Archaeological Museum, Konya, No. 796

offer sacrifice with the people. But when the apostles Barnabas and Paul heard of it, they tore their garments and rushed out among the multitude, crying, "Men, why are you doing this? We also are men, of like nature with you, and bring you good news, that you should turn from these vain things to a living God who made the heaven and the earth and the sea and all that is in them. In past generations he allowed all the nations to walk in their own ways; yet he did not leave himself without witness, for he did good and gave you from heaven rains and fruitful seasons, satisfying your hearts with food and gladness." With these words they scarcely restrained the people from offering sacrifice to them.

But Jews came there from Antioch and Iconium; and having persuaded the people, they stoned Paul and dragged him out of the city, supposing that he was dead. But when the disciples gathered about him, he rose up and entered the city.

Acts 14:8-20a

Lystra stands out for the miracle wrought on the lame man, deeply impressing the indigenous population. Scholars have been needlessly skeptical about this story because of several similar incidents recorded by St. Luke. The narrative, for instance, resembles St. Peter's healing of the lame man at the Beautiful Gate (Acts 3:2-8), but this account is so much more vividly and dramatically described than any other experience of St. Paul's first missionary journey, that St. Luke must have heard the story from an eyewitness. Such an eyewitness might have been Timothy, who was probably a native of Lystra and who later became St. Paul's faithful companion.

Anyone who has traveled through the villages and towns of the East has seen unfortunate cripples who drag themselves about in the dust and sit at the roadside begging. When the cripple was looked at intently by St. Paul, the same eyes fell upon him which fell upon Elymas, the sorcerer of Paphos. On this occasion, however, the penetrating glance of the Apostle saw that the cripple "had faith to be made well." As St. Peter had spoken to the lame man at the Beautiful Gate, so St. Paul commanded the cripple in Lystra to stand, and the cripple sprang up and walked. The Western Text adds some details, the most important being that the lame man was "in the fear of God," and that he was a pagan who had been converted to Judaism before he listened to St. Paul.

When the crowds saw what had happened, they believed that gods had descended in the likeness of men. They thought Barnabas was Zeus or Jupiter and Paul was Hermes or Mercury. Paul was the chief speaker and Mercury was known as the god of eloquence. St. John Chrysostomus and others believed that Barnabas had a tall and majestic appearance which would have suggested his identification as Jupiter. In Greek mythology these two gods were frequently represented as companions in their terrestrial expeditions. Of course, we cannot be certain that the Lycaonians of Lystra knew these legends, although if they did it would make their reaction more understandable.

The identification as gods was also suggested by local tradition, for the beautiful story of Philemon and Baucis was believed to have taken place near Lystra. Ovid, the last great Roman poet of the Augustan age, included the story in his *Metamorphoses* (viii, 618).

> Hither came Jupiter in the guise of a mortal, and with his father came Atlas' grandson (Mercury), he that bears the caduceus, his wings laid aside. To a thousand homes they came, seeking a place for rest; a thousand homes were barred against them. Still one house received them, humble indeed, thatched with straw and reeds from the marsh; but pious old Baucis and Philemon, of equal age, were in that cottage wedded in their youth, and in that cottage had grown old together.... And so when the heavenly ones came to this humble home and entered in at the lowly door, the old man set out a bench and bade them rest their limbs, while over this bench busy Baucis threw a rough covering.... The gods reclined. The old woman, with her skirts tucked up, with trembling hands set out the

table... olives, berries, cornel-cherries pickled in the lees of wine, endives, radishes, cream cheese and eggs and wine. Besides all this, pleasant faces were at the board and lively and abounding goodwill.

Finally Jupiter and Mercury revealed their identity and said "We are gods and this wicked neighbourhood shall be punished, but to you shall be given exemption. Leave your own dwelling and come with us to that tall mountain yonder." They both obeyed and when they turned around they saw the countryside covered with water except for their hut which was transformed into a temple which Philemon and Baucis served to the end of their lives. Their request to die at the same time so that neither would be left to mourn the other was granted and, having said farewell to each other, they fell asleep.

The news of St. Paul's wonderful healing spread rapidly through the city and the priest, or the priests according to the Western Text, of the Temple of Zeus hurried to fetch sacrificial bulls crowned with garlands. The Temple of Zeus at Lystra, as did the Temple of Artemis at Ephesus, stood outside the walls. An inscription "to Zeus before the city" has been found at Claudiopolis near Lystra. The attitude and behavior of the Apostles were characteristic and in line with rabbinical customs. Just as they had shaken off the dust in Pisidian Antioch to disassociate themselves from the pagan Antiochenes (Acts 13:51), so they tore their garments in the prescribed reaction against blasphemy (Mk 14:63). Only the outline of the Apostle's speech to the pagan audience is recorded. The Apostle's approach here is comparable to his approach to the Athenians in the famous Areopagus speech (Acts 17:22-31). Addressing the pagan Lycaonians and the philosophers of Athens he calls upon their experience and knowledge of God, Who at last had given a supreme revelation of Himself, and to turn "from these vain things to a living God."

St. Luke does not inform us about the Apostle's success in Lystra, but we know of at least one family, consisting of a grandmother, Lois, mother, Eunice, and son, Timothy, who accepted the Christian faith. Lois and Eunice were Jewesses (II

Tim. 1:5), although Eunice had married a Greek who had since died. Timothy, although not circumcised, probably had been raised in the Jewish faith. As mentioned above, the Jewish community in Lystra was small and it was not until Jews from Pisidian Antioch and Iconium arrived in the city that trouble arose. In II Corinthians 11:24-25, St. Paul recalls the experience when he states, "At the hands of the Jews. . . . once I was stoned" and in II Tim. 3:11 it is recorded, "What befell me at Antioch, at Iconium and at Lystra, what persecutions I endured."

No one would have guessed that a year later the Apostle would return to the city in which he had been stoned. On this second visit, at the beginning of his second missionary journey, Paul was accompanied by Silas. The two Apostles came from Antioch-on-the-Orontes over the Taurus Mountains through the pass known as the Cilician Gates into the Galatian part of Lycaonia, following Paul's former route in the reverse direction through Derbe, Lystra, and Iconium to Pisidian Antioch. Except for Lystra, we know nothing about St. Paul's experiences in these cities on his second visit, although we can be sure he and Silas were not in a hurry, nor were they inactive in Christ's service. The incident in Lystra concerns the circumcision of Timothy,

> the son of a Jewish woman who was a believer, but his father was a Greek. He was well spoken of by the brethren at Lystra and Iconium. Paul wanted Timothy to accompany him; and he took him and circumcised him because of the Jews that were in those places, for they all knew that his father was a Greek.
>
> Acts 16:1b-3

It is inconsistent for the same Apostle who wrote to the young churches in Galatia, "if you receive circumcision, Christ will be of no advantage to you" (Gal. 5:2), to circumcise a Galatian Christian, a member of the church to which he addressed the admonition. St. Paul was a missionary, however, not a systematician. He was a practical man; whatever furthered the preaching of the Word of God was consistent with his calling. As G.H.C. Macgregor said: "We cannot expect rigid consistency from one who could write: 'To the Jews I became a

Jew, in order to win Jews; to those under the law I became as one under the law. . . . I have become all things to all men, that I might by all means save some' " (I Cor. 9:20,22).

Derbe

> And on the next day he went on with Barnabas to Derbe. When they had preached the gospel to that city and had made many disciples. . .
>
> Acts 14:20b-21a

The town of Derbe was about sixty miles southeast of Lystra, but its exact location puzzled for many years those who have studied the topography of Lycaonia. Prof. J.R.S. Sterrett had placed Derbe 30 km. west of Karaman, while Sir William M. Ramsay had placed it still further west on the site of the modern village of Gudelisin. In 1956, however, at Kerti Hüyük, 22 km. northeast of Karaman, M. Ballance found a 2nd century A.D. inscription identifying the site of the town. The inscription was cut on a light limestone block which probably was used as a base for a large statue. The stone, which weighs about a ton, was found on the gently sloping skirt of a mound. Like the altar stone of Lystra, this relic of Derbe was removed from its original position at Kerti Hüyük to the Archaeological Museum in Konya, where it stands in the outer courtyard of the museum (No. 1146).

Kerti Hüyük, which is situated in the triangle formed by the villages of Beydilli, Aşiran, and Salur, is a mound approximately 900 feet long, 600 feet wide, and 60 feet high. M. Ballance mentions "that from the pottery on its surface it appears to have been still occupied in the Roman period." The importance of Derbe in antiquity was not very great, apart from a brief period of notoriety as the home of Cicero's friend Antipater. Nonetheless, it retained its name and identity until the 15th century, since it can probably be equated with the Dirvi mentioned in a supplement of 1465 to the vakfiye of the Imaret, the hospice for pilgrims, of Ibrahim Bey at Karaman.

Derbe was the Apostles' easternmost limit, and the only town in which they were not persecuted. St. Luke merely mentions that they preached the Gospel and made many disciples, although only one, Gaius of Derbe, is mentioned by name (Acts 20:4). From Derbe Paul and Barnabas could have traveled overland to Antioch-on-the-Orontes via the Cilician Gates, but instead they returned through Pisidian Antioch to the Pamphylian coast where they boarded a ship to reach Antioch-on-the-Orontes. The fact that they made many converts in Derbe suggests that the Apostles stayed there for some time, waiting perhaps until new magistrates had come into office in all of the cities from which they had been expelled.

The Return Journey

They returned to Lystra and to Iconium and to Antioch, strengthening the souls of the disciples, exhorting them to continue in the faith, and saying that through many tribulations we must enter the kingdom of God. And when they had appointed elders for them in every church, with prayer and fasting, they committed them to the Lord in whom they believed.

Acts 14:21b-23

They returned the way they had come in order to strengthen and organize the newly founded congregations in Lystra, Iconium, and Pisidian Antioch. In each city they appointed elders or presbyters, whose duties would have consisted of instructing the new converts and administering the infant fellowships.

Their first stopover was in Lystra where the Apostles may have stayed with Timothy, who was destined to become

St. Paul's faithful companion. From there they proceeded to Iconium and then to Pisidian Antioch. In each place St. Paul established a formal congregation, probably on the lines of the synagogue. The early history of most of these churches is clouded in darkness, although a few names have come down to us. Tradition informs us that not long after the visit of the Apostles, Eustochius, an idolater of Pisidian Antioch, was baptized and ordained a presbyter by Eudoxius. Eustochius later suffered martyrdom in Lystra. Aedesius, a pagan priest, was converted and ordained a presbyter by Optatus of Pisidian Antioch.

Then they passed through Pisidia, and came to Pamphylia.

Acts 14:24

According to the apocryphal Acts of Paul and Thecla, St. Paul went from Pisidian Antioch to the coastal town of Myra,

Side: Ancient Harbor

44

in the province of Lycia. Here Paul is said to have healed Hermocrates of dropsy and restored the sight to Hermippus, the older son of Hermocrates. A few years later, while being taken as a prisoner to Rome, the Apostle sailed on a ship of Adramyttium to Myra in Lycia, where he changed ships. In Myra the Apostle's guard "found a ship of Alexandria sailing for Italy" (Acts 27:5, 6). In the Christian world the town of Myra has reached fame through its 4th century bishop, St. Nicholas, whose generosity and kindness are remembered annually during the Christmas season. The legend of his surreptitious bestowal of dowries upon the three daughters of an impoverished citizen of Myra led to the identification of St. Nicholas with the giving of presents in secret. The father, unable to provide partners for his daughters, was on the point of giving them up to a life of shame when St. Nicholas intervened and saved the girls from sin. From Myra, so tradition informs us, the Apostle went to Side in Pamphylia, and "there was great sadness among the brethren that were in Pisidia and Pamphylia, because they yearned after his word and his holy appearance in Christ." A visit to Side was probable, for inscriptions testify that there were two synagogues in the town.

> And when they had spoken the word in Perga, they went down to Attalia....
>
> Acts 14:25

Before Paul and Barnabas left for Syrian Antioch they again stopped in Perga. This time they came for a definite purpose "to speak the word." We assume that they addressed the Jews in the synagogue of Perga as well as the Gentile population that worshiped Artemis Pergaia. From St. Luke's silence it appears that the preaching did not result in either conversions or persecutions, although tradition reports that Thrasymachus and Cleon with their wives Aline and Chrysa were converted and followed the Apostle. The Temple of Artemis in Perga, famous throughout Pamphylia, was in many ways as significant as that in Ephesus. Strabo relates that the temple stood on a height near the city, and that annual festivals were held there. The wealth of the sanctuary

is attested by Cicero's charges against Verres, whom he accused of having stolen the gold of Artemis Pergaia in collaboration with the Pergean physician Artemidoros in 79 B.C. Near the large theater was the almost 800 feet long stadium. The inner city, with its agora, gymnasium, and baths was fortified by a wall.

In 1838, Sir Charles Fellows, one of the earliest Western travelers to visit Perga before it was excavated, wrote of the site: "The first object that strikes the traveler on arriving here is the extreme beauty of the situation of the ancient town, lying between and upon the sides of two hills, with an extensive valley in front, watered by the river Cestrus and backed by the mountains of the Taurus." In his day, the ruins of the theater and stadium were used as an enclosure for nursing camels.

When the missionaries left they did not sail down the Cestrus River, but traveled across the plain to Attalia on the coast of the Pamphylian Gulf. Attalus II Philadelphus, king of Pergamum, had founded the city in the 2nd century B.C. From here they took a ship for Antioch-on-the-Orontes. It is a matter of conjecture, but since the Mediterranean was closed to navigation between early November and early March except for urgent domestic or international business, it seems likely that Paul and Barnabas would have returned to their base of Antioch-on-the-Orontes in the early autumn of 47.

> And from there they sailed to Antioch, where they had been commended to the grace of God for the work which they had fulfilled. And when they arrived, they gathered the church together and declared all that God had done with them, and how he had opened a door of faith to the Gentiles. And they remained no little time with the disciples.
>
> Acts 14:26-28

Perga: The Sea Gate

St. Luke does not tell us the kind of ship which the missionaries took. There were small coastal vessels as well as large sailing ships. Josephus mentions that one ship which sailed from Judaea to Italy carried as many as six hundred persons, and Pliny speaks of a ship that carried twelve hundred passengers in addition to cargo. Upon their arrival they accounted for their work. They had planted seeds of the faith among the Gentiles.

Antalya: The Ancient Harbor

EPHESUS

Glimpses of Ancient Ephesus

For centuries pilgrims from all corners of the ancient world assembled annually during the month of Artemision to offer their sacrifices to Artemis - Diana of Ephesus. The temple was one of the Seven Wonders of the world because of its unparalleled splendor and its monumental proportions. As one ancient writer said: "I have seen the walls and hanging gardens of Old Babylon, the statue of Olympian Jove, the Colossus of Rhodes, the great labor of the lofty Pyramids, and the ancient tomb of Mausolus. But when I beheld the Temple at Ephesus towering to the clouds, all these other marvels were eclipsed."

In its long history the Temple of Artemis was destroyed and rebuilt several times. The temple seen by the Apostle was the last of these reconstructions, completed in the first half of the 3rd century. St. Paul may well have known the story told by Strabo how, on the night Alexander the Great was born, Herostratus, a madman in search of fame, set the temple on fire. The Ephesians soon built a more splendid temple, having sold the pillars of the former temple and their personal belongings, including the jewelry of their women. Artemidorus adds that when Alexander visited Ephesus he offered to reimburse the citizens the cost of the temple on condition that his generosity be credited by an inscription. The Ephesians, however, were unwilling, and replied to the Macedonian king that it was inappropriate for a god to dedicate offerings to gods.

Pliny the Elder (23-79 A.D.), a contemporary of St. Paul, supplies our basic knowledge of the temple. Built on marshy

soil as a safeguard against earthquakes, the temple was 425 feet long and 225 feet wide. The 127 columns, 60 feet high, were each constructed by a different king. Of these, 36 were carved with elaborate reliefs. A large section of one of these reliefs has been preserved and is now in the British Museum in London. In 1965 Austrian archaeologists discovered the holy of holies of the later temple. It was a horseshoe shaped altar faced with marble and occupying a site 100 feet by 66 feet. According to Strabo, the Temple of Artemis was served by eunuch priests known as Megabyzi. They were held in great honor. Maidens assisted them in their priestly office. Priests known as Curetes were also attached to the service of Artemis.

According to an Ephesian legend the Curetes assisted Leto in giving birth to Artemis. There were also priests known as the Acrobatae who were found only in Ephesus and who walked on tiptoe. As were many other sanctuaries, the temple was a place of refuge offering shelter to criminals and runaway slaves. When Darius destroyed the temples of Asia, he spared those dedicated to Artemis. Persian emperor Darius, Macedonian conqueror Alexander, and Roman general Antony all paid homage to the glory of Diana.

The city of Ephesus also attracted many people of note because of its distinguished intellectual tradition. Apollonius of Tyana describes the city as "rich in the labors of its philosophers and rhetoricians, insomuch that it flourished, not so much by the strength of its cavalry, as by the number of its citizens devoted to science." Of the natives of Ephesus, Strabo writes, "Amongst the most celebrated of the ancients born at Ephesus are Heraclitus the obscure, and Hermodorus, who appears to have been the author of part of the Roman laws. The poet Hipponax was also of Ephesus as also the two painters Parrhasius and Apelles. Among the illustrious moderns of the city is reckoned the orator Alexander, called Lychnus." Whenever troubled by the Ephesians, St. Paul may well have remembered Heraclitus, the

Ephesus: Curetes Street

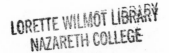
LORETTE WILMOT LIBRARY
NAZARETH COLLEGE

father of metaphysics, who wrote 500 years before that "the Ephesians all deserve to be hanged for having driven from their city Hermodorus, the most honest among them, saying, 'We will not have among us a good man, if any such there be, let him go and live elsewhere.' "

In 133 B.C. Attalus III of Pergamum bequeathed Ephesus to the Romans, who made it the capital of their province of Asia. During the war between Rome and Mithradates of Pontus the Ephesians revolted and massacred the Roman residents. Even those who had sought refuge in the temple sanctuary were dragged out and slain. The Roman general Sulla, after defeating Mithradates, punished Ephesus by imposing a heavy fine.

Not many years later, the Ephesians supported Antony and Octavian against Brutus and Cassius. After the latter were defeated, Antony came to Ephesus and imposed upon the city heavy taxes, much of which he spent to indulge his own extravagances. He identified himself with Bacchus and had Ephesian women dance before him as Bacchantes while the men and children played the roles of fauns and satyrs. When Cleopatra arrived in Cilicia, the rumor spread that "Venus had come to feast with Bacchus for the benefit of Asia," and when she entered Ephesus Antony allowed the citizens to hail her as queen.

Despite these dramatic events, Ephesus continued to grow into the most prosperous commercial center of western Anatolia and at one time had as many as 200,000 inhabitants. By the time of St. Paul's stay, the city of Diana had fully recovered, and controlled all the area's banking affairs. Despite the impression given the modern visitor, the city was not a center of prostitution or a cult center for the phallic deity, Bes. On this subject perhaps the reader will permit a digression.

As in most cities of the ancient world, there was a brothel in Ephesus. It was excavated by archaeologists from the Austrian Archaeological Institute, who also discovered a terracotta statue of the phallic deity, Bes. Both the brothel and the god Bes are exploited by the modern tourist industry although neither indicates that the Ephesian preoccupation with sex was in any way extraordinary.

That sex, however ancient, is good for business, is shown also by the popular interpretation of the graffiti on the western sidewalk of Marble Street, between the Mithradates Gate and the northern end of the Doric stoa. These graffiti can be divided into five subjects: the crowned female figure, the crosses, the inscription, the foot, and the so-called heart or pudendum.

The female figure is said to represent a courtesan who

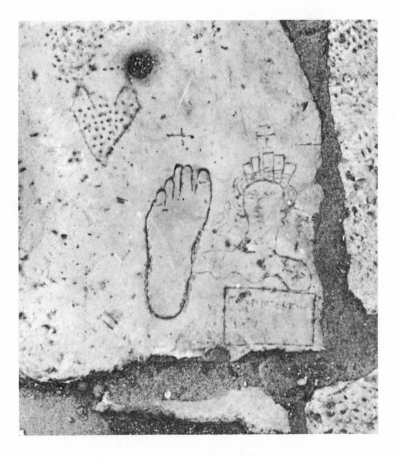

Ephesus: Graffiti on the Sidewalk of Marble Street

worked in the nearby brothel, but although representations of courtesans were frequent in the ancient world, few if any of them were crowned. Instead of a courtesan, it is more likely that the figure is a crude drawing of either the goddess Cybele or Tyche. The cross above the crown may have been drawn in the early Christian period. There are several very faint crosses above the figure to the left. Of the inscription only a few letters are legible, insufficient to help us date the graffiti or deduce its purpose.

The foot is usually said to indicate the direction of the brothel. Prostitutes in the ancient world are known to have advertised by wearing shoes with nails protruding from the soles and leaving the words "follow me." The drawing, however, upon closer examination appears to be of a male rather than a female foot. Imprints of two feet dating from the Roman period were found in the Shrine of Zeus Hypsistos in Athens. These feet are not a graffito, nor do we know their purpose. It is possible they were part of a votive offering, and that the Ephesian foot graffito was made for a similar purpose.

The triangular heart or pudendum as it is variously identified, has the most tenuous connection with the brothel. To begin with, there is no reason to think that it is an ancient graffito at all, and even if it were there is no evidence that the heart was a symbol of either love or sex in the ancient Roman world. Although phalli were frequently portrayed by the ancients, pudenda were not, being usually covered with shells or leaves, so this interpretation is equally unlikely. Furthermore, the triangle seems to be more recent than the other graffiti, and may even have been drawn to encourage the popular interpretation of these graffiti as an advertisement for the brothel.

Whether we accept the statement by St. Irenaeus, the 2nd century bishop of Lyons, that St. Paul founded the church in Ephesus, or the tradition that the church was founded in Ephesus when St. John settled with the Virgin Mary in the city immediately after Christ's ascension, there is no doubt that the Christian faith had reached Ephesus by the end of the first half of the 1st century. Unfortunately, the Acts of the Apostles does not provide us with an overall account of the growth and spread of the Gospel in the city of Ephesus or in the Roman province of Asia in general. In the days of St. Paul, the Roman province of Asia included merely the western part of what now is known as Asia Minor, just as the Roman province of Africa included only limited territory on the Mediterranean shore.

Forty-four verses of Acts are devoted to St. Paul's ministry in Ephesus. The purpose of St. Luke's Ephesian stories is to glorify his missionary hero for bringing the Word of God to all the residents of Asia, both Jews and Greeks (Acts 19:10). His ability to perform miracles was so immense that people approached him with handkerchiefs and aprons which, after he had touched them, were used to exorcise evil spirits. Jewish exorcists attempting to do the same failed hopelessly. The Apostle's success was so awe inspiring that many exorcists were readily won to Christ and consequently collected their books on magic for a public burning. St. Paul persuaded followers of many sectarian cults, including followers of St. John the Baptist, to the True Faith.

The last incident, depicted in detail by St. Luke, occurred in the large Ephesian theater where a riot ensued because of a certain Demetrius, a silversmith and maker of model shrines of Artemis, who felt his business interests threatened by the preaching of the Apostle.

The account in the Acts of the Apostles, though valuable and informative for our understanding of some isolated events of St. Paul's ministry, unfortunately lacks a coherent plan of his work and stay in the city of Diana. Ignored are his many trials and tribulations, forgotten are his deep concerns for his churches in Macedonia, Galatia, and Achaia. We are fortunate, therefore, that for the sake of a more complete account of St. Paul's work in Asia, we can turn to his own letters, many of which were composed during his stay in Ephesus. Although none of them contain a personal assessment of his Ephesian ministry, there are, nevertheless, sufficient references to his experience in Ephesus in his correspondence to his churches in Corinth, Galatia, Philippi, Colossae, and to Philemon from which we can reconstruct several important events of the Apostle's stay in this city.

St. Paul visited Ephesus twice. His first brief visit was at the end of his second missionary journey on his way from Corinth to Antioch. His second stay lasted for a period of three years during which time the Christian church was either established or strengthened. Finally, at the end of his third missionary journey, he met once more with the elders of the Ephesian church in the port of Miletus.

St. Paul's First Visit to Ephesus

And they came to Ephesus, and he left them there; but he himself went into the synagogue and argued with the Jews. When they asked him to stay for a longer period, he declined; but on taking leave of them he said, "I will return to you if God wills," and he set sail from Ephesus.

Acts 18:19-21

After twenty months of strenuous labor in Corinth, the capital of Achaia, St. Paul and his fellow tentmakers, Aquila and Priscilla, crossed from Cenchreae, the eastern harbor of Corinth, to Ephesus. The wait for a ship would not have been long, for no voyage across the Aegean was more frequently made than that between the two flourishing capitals and mercantile centers of the Roman provinces of Achaia and Asia, Corinth and Ephesus. The trip was made in the autumn of 51. Sailing from Corinth, the ship passed the northern Cyclades Islands before entering the Bay of Ephesus. While Cicero informs us that it took him fifteen days to reach the coast of Asia Minor from Corinth, other ancient writers speak of a three or four day sail. An impressive sight must have unfolded itself before the eyes of the Apostle as the ship approached the city from the west and entered the wide mouth of the Cayster River. The shoreline has moved since St. Paul's time, for today there is no harbor and Ephesus looks as though it were an inland city. Strabo, writing thirty years before the arrival of St. Paul in Ephesus, gives us a detailed description of the harbor of Ephesus. The harbor was shallow because of silting from the Cayster River. King Attalus Philadelphus, wishing the harbor to accommodate large cargo vessels, ordered a mole to be constructed, but this held more silt in the harbor and made it even more shallow. Remains of a stone embankment identified as this mole were discovered between 1863 and 1874 by J.T. Wood in the course of his excavations at Ephesus.

Disembarking at Port Coressus, the harbor of Ephesus, the Apostle, Aquila, and Priscilla would have passed through the magnificent Harbor Gate at the western end of the main road leading to the theater. This wide marble paved artery, some 1,700 feet long, later became known as the Arcadian Way in honor of the emperor Arcadius (383-408 A.D.) who enlarged and restored it. Both sides of this road were lined by colonnades, behind which were storerooms and shops. An inscription found among the ruins informs us that in the 4th century the Arcadian Way was lighted at night by lanterns. At one intersection of the Arcadian Way with a side street there stood a tetrapylon similar to that at Gerasa in Palestine. The decorative columns of the tetrapylon were probably surmounted by statues of the four evangelists. To the north of this road was the Roman agora, where many Roman inscriptions and several statues were unearthed. To the south was the spacious Hellenistic agora, surrounded by porticoes with shops. A waterclock stood in its center.

Three monumental gates led into the agora, the East Gate, the West Gate, and the South Gate known as the Gate of Mazeus and Mithradates. In 17 A.D. Ephesus, like Sardis, Magnesia, and most cities of Western Asia, was destroyed by a terrible earthquake. The emperor Tiberius (14-37 A.D.) began the work of restoration, and later Hadrian (117-138 A.D.) did much to rebuild the city. Many of the buildings, therefore, which may now be seen in Ephesus, were not standing in the days of the Apostle. The famous Gymnasium of Vedius, dedicated to Artemis and the Emperor Antoninus Pius (138-161 A.D.), was built in the 2nd century, as were the Baths also known as Constan-

tine's Baths, since they were restored during the reign of Constantine. Similarly, the Library of Celsus at the end of Marble Street, the monumental Temple of Serapis with its vast portico, and the elegant little Odeion had not been built in St. Paul's day. The majority of the monuments visible today were built in the 2nd century A.D. or even later.

At the time of St. Paul's travels there were large Jewish communities in all the principal cities of the Roman provinces of Asia and Galatia. Many Jews left Babylon about 200 B.C. and settled in places like Akmonia, Sebaste, Eumenia, Apamea, Laodicea, Miletus, and Ephesus. The Talmud referred to these Jews as the Ten Tribes, although "the baths and the wines" — the luxurious Roman life — had separated them from their brethren. Josephus informs us that the Syrian ruler Antiochus II Theos (261-247 B.C.) had granted the Jews of Ionia full citizenship. In the 1st century B.C. the Ionians sought to deprive the Jews of this privilege, but the Roman official Marcus Agrippa refused the petition and thus safeguarded the rights of the Jews. In Ephesus the Jews enjoyed many privileges which, according to Josephus, were granted them by Dolabella, the governor. Those Jews who were Roman citizens were exempted from military service, and they were permitted to maintain their customs and live in accordance to their laws. The decree of the people of Ephesus stated:

> In the presidency of Menophilus, on the first of the month Artemision, the following decree was passed by the people on the motion of the magistrates, and was announced by Nicanor. Whereas the Jews in the city have petitioned the proconsul Marcus Junius Brutus, son of Pontius, that they might observe their Sabbath and do all those things which are in accordance with their native customs without interference from anyone, and the governor has granted their request, it has therefore been decreed by the council and

Ephesus: Arcadian Way

people that as the matter is of concern to the Romans, no one shall be prevented from keeping the Sabbath days nor be fined for so doing.

Before the destruction of the Jewish Temple in Jerusalem in 70 A.D., Roman law even stipulated that the Jews constituted an autonomous community. Thus, for example, in Alexandria they had their own ethnarch as the head of their community.

We do not know exactly where the Ephesus synagogue was located but there is no question that it existed. It was probably on the northern outskirts of the city in order to be near water necessary for ritual purposes. During his first short stay, St. Paul visited the local synagogue, probably on the Sabbath when the people were assembled. As in Pisidian Antioch, the curiosity of those assembled was aroused, but the departure of St. Paul's ship for Syria prevented him from staying on. The Western Text explains the Apostle's decision to leave Ephesus, "I must by all means keep this feast that comes in Jerusalem" (Acts 18:21). The voyage to Caesarea in the autumn could be long and dangerous, and it is possible that in the course of it one of St. Paul's shipwrecks may have taken place (II Cor. 11:25).

Aquila and Priscilla remained in Ephesus where they became pillars of the Christian community. Originally from the Roman province of Pontus on the shores of the Euxine, Aquila, a Jew, and his Roman wife, Priscilla, had settled in Rome from which they were expelled during the reign of the emperor Claudius. In the *Life of Claudius* by the Roman historian Suetonius we read that "the Jews, who by the instigation of one Chrestos were evermore tumultuous, he banished from Rome." The 5th century Spanish historian, Paulus Orosius, informs us that expulsion occurred in the ninth year of the reign of Claudius, i.e. between January 25th, 49 and January 24th, 50. It was during this period, therefore, that Aquila and Priscilla arrived in Corinth where they met St. Paul. St. Luke tells us that St. Paul

Ephesus: Theater and Hellenistic Agora

went to see them because they were tentmakers, as was he, and he stayed and worked with them (Acts 18:2,3). This friendship soon resulted in Aquila and Priscilla accompanying St. Paul to Asia. H.V. Morton suggests that "this husband and wife left Corinth for Ephesus at the call of more profitable work" since Ephesus was famous for the manufacture of luxurious tents and marquees. Other scholars have maintained that St. Paul returned to Syria because of poor health and that Aquila and Priscilla accompanied the Apostle in order to assist him. This may also be the reason why the account in Acts of St. Paul's journey from Corinth via Ephesus to Syria is so brief. St. Luke, the narrator, was a physician bound by the Hippocratic oath which stipulated that "whatsoever I shall see or hear in the course of my profession, as well as outside my profession in my intercourse with men, if it be what should not be published abroad, I will never divulge, holding such things to be holy secrets." Notwithstanding these points, it is most probable that Aquila and Priscilla went to Ephesus to prepare for St. Paul's future ministry there, for eventually, one of the congregations in Ephesus met in their house (Rom. 16:5). This unusual couple was deeply committed to the Lord Jesus Christ. The Apostle faced many difficulties while preaching the Gospel in Ephesus, and at least once Aquila and Priscilla "risked their necks" for him (Rom. 16:3, 4).

Apollos In Ephesus

Now a Jew named Apollos, a native of Alexandria, came to Ephesus. He was an eloquent man, well versed in the scriptures. He had been instructed in the way of the Lord; and being fervent in spirit, he spoke and taught accurately the things concerning Jesus, though he knew only the baptism of John. He began to speak boldly in the synagogue; but when Priscilla and Aquila heard him, they took him and expounded to him the way of God more accurately. And when he wished to cross to Achaia, the brethren encouraged him, and wrote to the disciples to receive him. When he arrived, he greatly helped those who through grace had believed, for he powerfully confuted the Jews in public, showing by the scriptures that the Christ was Jesus.

Acts 18:24-28

An Alexandrian Jew, who was well read in the Old Testament and a good speaker, came to Ephesus during St. Paul's absence. His name was Apollos or, as the Western Text calls him, Apollonius. St. Luke's description of the theology of Apollos has led many people to wonder whether or not he was a Christian and, if so, where he had obtained his knowledge of the Christian faith. Since "he had been instructed in the way of the Lord" he knew something about Christian beliefs, for "he spoke and taught accurately the things concerning Jesus," and yet he had not received Christian baptism. "He knew only the baptism of John" meant that he had been baptized with water as a symbol of repentence, though he was not baptized in the name of Jesus.

When St. Paul returned to Ephesus he found there "some disciples" who had never heard of the Holy Spirit and who were baptized "into John's baptism" (Acts 19:1-7). In view of these passages there is sufficient reason to think that a "John the Baptist sect" existed apart from or perhaps even in rivalry with the Christian church. Apollos recognized Jesus as the Christ, he knew of His earthly ministry and probably the resurrection, yet he knew nothing of Pentecost and the gift of the Holy Spirit.

Priscilla and Aquila, who had listened to him speak in the Ephesian synagogue, were impressed but also concerned about his lack of understanding of the power of the Holy Spirit, so "they took him and expounded to him the way of God more accurately." Realizing that his knowledge of the Old Testament would make him a formidable disputant with the Jews and that his knowledge of philosophy would enable him to argue with the Greeks, Priscilla and Aquila may well have suggested that he sail to Corinth. We must assume that they baptized him in the name of Jesus before he left, for baptism in His name was the seal of discipleship. Aquila and Priscilla gave him a letter of introduction for the disciples in Corinth, and he became so popular there that partisans collected about him (I Cor. 1:12; 3:4, 22; 4:6). These partisans probably contrasted his brilliance and eloquence with the plain and simple style of preaching adopted by St. Paul when in Corinth. When Apollos realized the schismatic effects of his ministry, he left Corinth and returned to Ephesus where he was when St. Paul wrote I Cor. 16:12. The Apostle urged him to return to Corinth, "but it was not at all his will to come now" (I Cor. 16:12).

St. Paul's Second Visit to Ephesus

> After spending some time there (in Syrian Antioch) he departed and went from place to place through the region of Galatia and Phrygia, strengthening all the disciples.... While Apollos was at Corinth, Paul passed through the upper country and came to Ephesus
>
> Acts 18:23, 19:1a.

After his brief visit in Ephesus in the autumn of 51, St. Paul reembarked for Caesarea. Then "he went up and greeted the church and then went down to Antioch" (Acts 18:22). St. Luke does not tell us exactly where the Apostle went in Syria, but "going up" was frequently used to mean visiting Jerusalem, 2,300 feet above sea level. Antioch was his base, the center of Gentile Christianity, so it is only natural that he set out from there on his third missionary journey.

Some scholars maintain that St. Paul left Syrian Antioch in the summer of 53. The most natural route would have led via Tarsus through the Cilician Gates to Derbe, Lystra, Iconium, and Pisidian Antioch where "he strengthened all the disciples" who had accepted the Christian faith during his first missionary journey. From Pisidian Antioch he may have gone to Apamea, which had the largest Jewish community in Phrygia, and then on to Colossae and Laodicea in the Lycus Valley. From Laodicea he may have traveled down the River Meander — which has contributed a verb to the English language — to Ephesus. When he arrived he was welcomed by Aquila and Priscilla, who must have told him about the cultured Alexandrian Jew, Apollos, and the followers of John the Baptist.

> There he found some disciples. And he said to them, "Did you receive the Holy Spirit when you believed?" And they said, "No, we have never even heard that there is a Holy Spirit." And he said, "Into what then were you baptized?" They said, "Into John's baptism." And Paul said, "John baptized with the baptism of repentance, telling the people to believe in the one who was to come after him, that is, Jesus." On hearing this, they were baptized in the name of the Lord Jesus. And when Paul had laid his hands upon them, the Holy Spirit came on them; and they spoke with tongues and prophesied. There were about twelve of them in all.
>
> Acts 19:1b-7.

As mentioned before, there was a sectarian following of John the Baptist in Ephesus, of which Apollos was probably the principal spokesman. St. Luke calls its members "disciples," and whether or not they were Christians in the apostolic sense of the term has been much debated. St. Paul did not hesitate to rebaptize them in the name of the Lord Jesus. When Paul laid his hands upon them they received the Holy Spirit. As Moses, when appointing Joshua his successor, laid his hands on him (Numbers 27:23), so the Apostles had used this rite of baptizing, healing, confirming, and ordaining. Speaking "with tongues" and prophesying referred to the outpouring of inarticulate sounds under the stress of an overpowering religious experience. Although he accepted the practice of glossalia, St. Paul did not consider it one of the more important divine gifts (I Cor. 12:4-11, 14:1-40), and he implied that it was among the "childish ways" which are to be outgrown (I Cor. 13:8-11).

St. Paul's Preaching to the Jews and the Residents of Asia

> And he entered the synagogue and for three months spoke boldly, arguing and pleading about the kingdom of God; but when some were stubborn and disbelieved, speaking evil of the Way before the congregation, he withdrew from them, taking the disciples with him, and argued daily in the hall of Tyrannus. This continued for two years, so that all the residents of Asia heard the word of the Lord, both Jews and Greeks.
>
> Acts 19:8-10.

St. Paul had argued in the synagogue with the Jews during his first brief visit to Ephesus. Approximately three years later, in the autumn of 54, he returned to the synagogue and spoke of the Kingdom of God. The idea of a messianic Kingdom was familiar to the Jews, but for St. Paul it was through Jesus, the true Christ, that this Kingdom was to be ushered in and established. In Corinth and in some other places the whole Jewish community had rejected the Apostle. Ephesus was like most cities in which the Apostle preached, for only "some were stubborn and disbelieved," though they included the leaders of the synagogue.

The reference to the "Way" is interesting. The early believers and their pagan contemporaries used this term to describe the followers of Jesus, although it seems first to have been used by the enemies of the disciples to mark them as a sect. Before his conversion, Saul used it while preparing to travel to Damascus, "so that if he found any belonging to the Way. . . he might bring them bound to Jerusalem" (Acts 9:2). Felix and Herod Agrippa also were familiar with the name, upon which the believers themselves looked with favor. The prophets had dignified the term. Isaiah had sung of the highway of holiness:

And a highway shall be there, and it shall be called the

Holy Way; the unclean shall not pass over it, and fools
shall not err therein.

Isaiah 35:8

After three months of preaching, St. Paul was evicted from
the synagogue, but fortunately he was able to use the hall of
Tyrannus, which was probably rented to visiting lecturers. The
hall of Tyrannus played the same part in Ephesus as did·the
house of Titus Justus adjoining the synagogue in Corinth. To
strangers in Ephesus the Apostle would have appeared as one
of those numerous traveling philosophers who went from town
to town sharing their wisdom. The Western Text is more explicit
and tells us that St. Paul taught "from the fifth to the tenth hour,"
that is from 11 A.M. until 4 P.M. after business hours during the
heat ot the day.

As did other artisans and tradesmen, St. Paul would have
begun his daily work as a tentmaker before sunrise and continued
until closing time before noon. In his speech to the Ephesisn
elders he reminded them that "you yourselves know that these
hands ministered to my necessities" (Acts 20:34) and in I Corinthians 4:12 he alluded to his work, "We labor, working with
our own hands." Sir William M. Ramsay mentions that "public
life in the Ionian cities ended regularly at the fifth hour; and we
may add to the facts elsewhere stated a regulation at Attalia in
Lycia that public distribution of oil should be from the first to
the fifth hour." After 11 A.M. the Apostle would have been free
to devote himself to the missionary work which was the primary
purpose of his stay in Ephesus. He kept this schedule, undoubt-
edly with many unforeseen interruptions, for two years.

During this time, through the Apostle's preaching, Christian congregations were established throughout the province of
Asia. Congregations were established at Colossae (Col. 2:1)
and Hierapolis (Col. 4:13) as well as in the "seven churches" of
the Apocalypse: Ephesus, Smyrna, Pergamum, Thyatira, Sardis,
Philadelphia, Laodicea. We do not know if St. Paul visited the
cities mentioned. Perhaps he did not, but people from these
cities came to Ephesus to hear him and then organized congregations in their own cities. Christian churches were well estab-

lished in the Roman province of Asia by the latter part of the 1st century.

St. Paul probably traveled down the Lycus Valley on his way from Pisidian Antioch to Ephesus, and he may well have stopped at Laodicea, Colossae, and Hierapolis. Colossae stood on a small hill south of the Lycus River. The pagan gods Isis and Serapis, together with Helios, Demeter, Selene, and the Ephesian Artemis were worshipped there. The leader of the Christian community in Colossae was Epaphras "our beloved fellow servant" (Col. 1:7). Epaphras, moreover, had been active in the evangelization of the two other cities of the Lycus Valley, Hierapolis and Laodicea (Col. 4:13). Later, while in prison in Ephesus, St. Paul addressed a circular letter to the Colossians which they were to share with the Christians in Laodicea.

Laodicea was twelve miles west of Colossae. The city was refounded and named by Antiochus II for his sister-wife Laodice in 250 B.C. Though for centuries deserted, Laodicea was never completely forgotten. When Thomas Smith, the first modern traveler to describe it, visited Laodicea in the spring of 1671, its identity was unquestioned. In the 18th century, Robert Chandler wrote a fuller description, which is still useful, for the Society of Dilettanti. It was excavated between 1961 and 1963 by archaeologists from Laval University of Quebec. The most conspicuous remains are the well preserved stadium, the massive structures of the gymnasium, and the blocks from the eastern gate.

A large Jewish colony must have lived there, for in 62 B.C. when the propraetor Flaccus seized the gold the Jews in Laodicea had collected for the Temple of Jerusalem, he found that it weighed more than twenty pounds. According to Josephus, the Jewish community in Laodicea was permitted to observe the Sabbath and perform other rites according to their laws. In 50 B.C. Cicero, while serving as governor of Asia, stayed in Laodicea for ten weeks. Laodicea had a well-known medical center which had been established by Zeuxis and was later directed by Alexander Philalethes. Is it possible that St. Luke received his medical training in Laodicea? The fact that his name appears in the salutations to the church in Colossae and to Philemon of Laodicea (Col. 4:14, Philemon 24) suggests that he was known to the Christians of these two congregations.

The church in Laodicea met in the house of Nympha (Col. 4:15) just as in Ephesus the church met in the house of Aquila and Priscilla (I Cor. 16:19, Rom. 16:5) and in Corinth in the house of Gaius (Rom. 16:23). We must assume that the Christian congregation in Laodicea, as did most of the other churches in Asia, consisted of both Jews and Gentiles. At any rate, the church in Laodicea was one of the "seven churches" to which St. John wrote the well-known words:

> I know your works: you are neither cold nor hot. Would that you were cold or hot! So, because you are luke-warm, and neither cold nor hot, I will spew you out of my mouth.... Those whom I love, I reprove and chasten, so be zealous and repent. Behold, I stand at the door and knock; if any one hears my voice and opens the door, I will come in to him and eat with him, and he with me.
>
> Rev. 3:15-16, 19-20.

The third city in the Lycus Valley in which Epaphras had been active was Hierapolis, known today as Pamukkale. The city had been founded in the 2nd century B.C. by Eumenes II, King of Pergamum, and was damaged as was Ephesus in the earthquake of 17 A.D. The Christian church here also may have developed out of the local synagogue, for Hierapolis as well had a large Jewish community. According to the apocryphal Acts of Philip, the church in Hierapolis met in the house of Stachys. Here Philip, his sister Mariamne, and Bartholomew proclaimed the Word of God and healed and converted Nicanora, the Jewish wife of the Roman proconsul. Philip eventually suffered martyrdom in Hierapolis, and recently a striking 5th century martyrium of St. Philip was discovered. The martyrium was used for commemorative services on the saint's feast day. One of the foremost apostolic fathers, Papias, "a hearer of John and the associate of Polycarp of Smyrna," lived in Hierapolis. Papias's *Exposition of the Lord's Oracles* is the principal early authority concerning the Gospels of St. Matthew and St. Mark.

The people of Smyrna, now called Izmir, would have come in touch with St. Paul and the members of his Ephesian congregation during visits to the provincial capital. In the Roman period Smyrna was the seat of a conventus which included south Aeolis and a greater part of the Hermus Valley. We do not know when the church at Smyrna was founded, but it existed from a very early time. The city's large and influential Jewish community 'must have caused serious troubles for Christians, accusing them before the Roman authorities. Half a century after St. Paul's ministry in Asia, John, the Seer of Patmos, wrote the church in Smyrna:

> I know your tribulation and your poverty (but you are rich) and the slander of those who say that they are Jews and are not, but are a synagogue of Satan.
>
> Rev. 2:9

The next verse contains the sentence which inspired Christians for centuries to come: "Be faithful until death, and I will give you the crown of life" (Rev. 2:10b). In the 2nd century the young church in Smyrna suffered terrible persecutions, culminating in the martyrdom of its prominent early bishop, Polycarp, who was killed in 155 A.D.

About 110 km. north of Smyrna was Pergamum, or Bergama as it is called today. Although most New Testament documents were written on papyrus, it is possible that St. Paul's correspondence from Ephesus may have been written on the new writing material, parchment or *charta pergamena,* which was invented in Pergamum in the 2nd century B.C. at a time when the Egyptians were refusing to export papyrus. The city was also famous for its Temple of Zeus decorated with a series of magnificent bas-reliefs, its theater, its library, and its asklepeion. Some of the people of Pergamum must have visited Ephesus and heard the preaching of St. Paul. From St. John's letter addressed to the church in Pergamum we learn that Antipas, the spiritual leader of the Pergamum congregation, was killed during severe persecutions. The members of the church are commended for their steadfastness in the face of difficulties.

I know where you dwell, where Satan's throne is; you hold fast my name and you did not deny my faith even in the days of Antipas my witness, my faithful one, who was killed among you, where Satan dwells.

Rev. 2:13

Most scholars have identified "Satan's throne" with the city of Pergamum, which was the principal center of the imperial cult under the early empire in the province of Asia. Others have thought the phrase alluded specifically to the monumental Pergamum altar of Zeus built by Eumenes II (197-159 B.C.) which stood at the end of the western terrace of the acropolis overlooking the Selinus River and the asklepeion. In the latter part of the 19th century the altar was transferred to Berlin where a special museum was built for it. As did the churches in Corinth and Galatia, so also the congregation of Pergamum suffered from sectarianism and immorality. In his admonition to those who engaged in idolatry (Rev. 2:13-17) St. John was in full agreement with St. Paul who had warned the Corinthians not to partake of the sacred meals of the pagans (I Cor. 10:14-22, 11:30).

The fourth letter of the Apocalypse (Rev. 2:18-29) was addressed to the church of Thyatira, today the town of Akhisar which, according to Strabo, was a settlement of Macedonians. Lydia, St. Paul's first convert in Philippi, was a native of Thyatira, where a Jewish colony is thought to have existed since she was described as "a worshiper of God" (Acts 16:14). In the days of St. Paul, Apollo Tyrimnaios, who was worshiped together with the emperors, was the tutelary deity of this city. We have no evidence that St. Paul visited Thyatira, although some Thyatirans probably visited Ephesus and were converted by his preaching. The members of this church also are commended for their works, love, faith, service, and patient endurance, but again praise is followed by blame. False prophets had split the congregation and idolatry, particularly emperor worship, had undermined the fellowship.

Sardis was the capital of ancient Lydia and an important city in Asia. It was destroyed by the earthquake in 17 A.D. but

rebuilt through the generosity of the emperor Tiberius. The Jewish community, from which the Christians may have sprung, enjoyed more privileges in Sardis than in most cities of Asia. In a decree by the people of Sardis it was stipulated that the Jews

> May in accordance with their accepted customs come together and have a communal life and adjudicate suits among themselves, and that a place be given them in which they may gather together and offer their ancestral prayers and sacrifices to God... and that a place be set apart by the magistrates for them to build and inhabit, such as they may consider suitable for this purpose, and that the market officials shall be charged with the duty of having suitable food for them brought in.

There are no traces of a synagogue dating to the time of St. Paul. The Sardis synagogue, excavated in 1963 by American archaeologists, existed from the 2nd to the 7th century A.D. St. John addressed one of his strongest admonitions to the Christians in Sardis, accusing them of being spiritually dead.

> I know your works; you have the name of being alive, and you are dead. Awake, and strengthen what remains and is on the point of death, for I have not found your works perfect in the sight of my God.
>
> Rev. 3:1-2

All, however, were not guilty, for

> Yet you have still a few names in Sardis, people who have not soiled their garments; and they shall walk with me in white, for they are worthy.
>
> Rev. 3:4

Pergamum: Altar Base from the Temple of Zeus

The wine center of Philadelphia, where Dionysus was worshiped, the modern town of Alaşehir, was between Sardis and Laodicea. In 17 and again in 23 A.D. the town was destroyed by earthquake but, as was Thyatira, it was rebuilt by Tiberius. Here as elsewhere the Christian congregation probably emerged out of the synagogue.

We have no scriptural evidence for the founding of Christian congregations in the other towns and cities of the province of Asia. If, however, "all the residents of Asia heard the word of the Lord, both Jews and Greeks," we have every reason to assume that in the 1st century communities of Christians were also established in cities such as Magnesia-on-the-Meander, Tralles, Antioch-on-the-Meander, Aphrodisias, Troy, Scepsis, and Assos.

St. Paul's Ministry to the Church in Corinth

The Apostle did not restrict his ministry to the spoken word while in Ephesus, for several of the most important apostolic documents were written during his stay in the city. One day, while working as usual at his trade, he received some visitors from Corinth. St. Paul referred to them as "Chloe's people." They may have been her slaves, freedmen, or employees. The news they delivered to the Apostle was disturbing. The Christians in Corinth were breaking up into factions about their favorite teachers, one of whom was Apollos, the eloquent Alexandrian Jewish convert, who since had returned to Ephesus. Even more serious were the incidents of immoral conduct reported by Chloe's people. The Corinthian Christians had turned to pagan courts for the settlement of their business disagreements and, far more serious yet, their celebration of the Lord's Supper had degenerated into a carouse.

On hearing these reports, what could the Apostle do? He had already written one letter to the church in Corinth (I Cor.

5:9-13). Not much later three members of the congregation, Stephanas, Achaicus, and Fortunatus had come to him in Ephesus (I Cor. 16:17) with a letter (I Cor. 7:1) asking about such matters as the relationship between the sexes, the meaning of marriage, engagement, and divorce. Another question of deep concern dealt with the purchase of meat from animals sacrificed at pagan shrines. They wondered if the purchase of such meat necessarily meant the support of pagan cults. They wondered how people were to conduct themselves in church and if women should wear veils in church. They also wanted the advice of the Apostle about the practice of speaking in tongues.

St. Paul replied to all of these issues in detail in a letter he dispatched with Timothy to Corinth and which later became known as the First Letter to the Corinthians. In his closing remarks of this letter he mentioned his desire to visit Corinth, and he shared with them his plans to visit Macedonia, but at the same time he was determined "to stay in Ephesus until Pentecost, for a wide door for effective work has opened to me, and there are many adversaries" (I Cor. 16:8-9).

St. Paul interrupted his stay in Ephesus at least once to travel to Corinth. This was after he had written his First Letter to the Corinthians, which apparently did not restore the peace within the church at Corinth. False teachers from the outside had attempted to undermine St. Paul's influence and under their guidance a member of the Corinthian church had become especially antagonistic to the Apostle. But when he repented, St. Paul forgave him and called upon his Corinthian brethren to do the same (II Cor. 2:5-8). While the rebellion against the Apostle was still going on St. Paul sailed from Ephesus directly to Cenchreae, the eastern port of Corinth, to deal in person with his opponents, but he was unsuccessful. Disappointed, he returned to Ephesus to resume his work among the Ephesian Christians.

The problems of the church in Corinth remained on his mind. He could not accept defeat and the only alternative was to address another letter to the Corinthian Christians. They had accused him of being humble in face-to-face contacts while in Corinth but bold in his distance from them. He denied the accusation and reminded them that his authority was derived from God. Known as the "severe letter," this document is incorporated in II Cor. 10-13. Titus, who at that time was staying in Ephesus, delivered the "severe letter" to the Corinthians and later met the Apostle in Macedonia with the good news of the church's repentance.

St. Paul Writes to the Churches of Galatia

Ephesus with its Temple of Artemis, "she whom all Asia and the world worship" (Acts 19:27b), attracted people from all over Asia Minor for religious and business purposes. Among the numerous visitors from the province of Galatia were Christians who informed the Apostle that Jewish Christians known as Judaizers were preaching a narrow and legalistic type of Christianity among the churches St. Paul had organized a few years earlier, and that some of the Galatian Christians had embraced the new faith. As we have seen, St. Paul's mission in the cities of Pisidian Antioch, Iconium, Lystra, and Derbe had been fruitful. He had revisited these congregations on his second journey. He knew the churches well and was particularly attached to them through Timothy of Lystra who had become his most faithful helper and companion. These Judaizers were legalists, who maintained that one had to be a descendant of Abraham, or become one by embracing Judaism and being circumcised in order to benefit from the spiritual blessings of Jesus Christ. The only way to enter the church, they argued, was through the synagogue. Christianity as they understood it was a messianic Judaism. Moreover, these Jewish minded teachers had attacked St. Paul and questioned his authority to proclaim the Gospel, especially to the uncircumcised, the Gentiles. Since he had not been with Jesus he did not possess full apostolic authority, and thus they charged him with being a mere opportunist, who observed the Law in Jerusalem, but when he thought it would profit him, he was ready not to insist on circumcision.

This, in brief, was the situation confronting the Apostle.

St. Paul realized that he could not leave Ephesus, although he wrote to the Galatians "I could wish to be present with you now and to change my tone, for I am perplexed about you" (Gal. 4:20). Along with the churches of Macedonia, Achaia, and Asia, the Galatian Christians constituted the fourth group which retained a close relationship with the Apostle. Instead of visiting them, however, he wrote "the churches in Galatia" (Gal. 1:2b), meaning his congregations in Pisidian Antioch, Iconium, Lystra, and Derbe, a circular letter which is one of the most remarkable documents in the New Testament. On his first visit, he wrote, they had received him with a hospitality and kindness which had touched him deeply. They had treated him as an "angel of God, as Christ Jesus" (Gal. 4:14b). They would have plucked out their own eyes to give him (Gal. 4:15b). Now, they had turned from the liberty of the Gospel to the old bondage of custom and tradition. This is the most impetuous of St. Paul's letters. As Professor Edgar J. Goodspeed says, "its vigor, variety, audacity, and self-revealing frankness, together with its direct insight into religious truth, put it in a class by itself among the books of the New Testament." For St. Paul, the Galatians were his children, whom he could not permit to fall into blindness and folly. Dictated in a hurry, the letter was written by one of the many scribes who existed in every major town, and signed by the Apostle with large letters at the end (Gal. 6:11).

St. Paul's Imprisonment in Ephesus

Although St. Luke does not mention that the Apostle was imprisoned in Ephesus during his two to three year stay in the city, St. Paul referred repeatedly to his sufferings in his correspondence with the churches in Achaia, Macedonia, and Asia. We do not know the charge which led to St. Paul's imprisonment. Professor G.S. Duncan of the University of St. Andrews suggested that the Ephesian Jews had built up a singularly ingenious case against St. Paul, charging him with diverting sums

of money which normally would have been sent as the annual contribution to Jerusalem. The Jews approached Junius Silanus, the Roman governor, and persuaded him to imprison St. Paul. While stationed in Ephesus, Junius Silanus became the first poison victim of Nero's reign because Agrippina, Nero's mother, saw him as a potential rival to her son.

Writing to the church in Corinth, St. Paul said, "For we do not want you to be ignorant, brethren, of the affliction we experienced in Asia; for we were so utterly, unbearably crushed that we despaired of life itself. Why, we felt that we had received the sentence of death...." (II Cor. 1:8-9a), and on another occasion he referred to his fighting with beasts at Ephesus (I Cor. 15:32). The apocryphal Acts of Paul have elaborated on the Apostle's imprisonment. The Ephesians had become angered by St. Paul's speech and had imprisoned him until he would be fed to the lions. Eubola and Artemilla, wives of eminent Ephesian men, visited St. Paul in the prison at night, "desiring the grace of the divine washing." Miraculously, St. Paul's iron fetters were loosed and, unrecognized, he went with his two disciples to the seashore where he baptized them. Then he returned to the prison without any of the guards knowing he had gone.

Another passage in the Acts of Paul comments on the Apostle's statement of having fought with beasts at Ephesus. The apocryphal story tells us that "a lion of huge size and unmatched strength was let loose upon St. Paul, and it ran to him in the stadium and lay down at his feet." Neither the lion nor any of the other savage beasts touched him. Finally, a violent hailstorm poured down and "shattered the heads" of many men and beasts, saving the Apostle's life. Gladiator shows and contests were well known in Ephesus for they had been introduced into the Roman province of Asia by Lucullus in 70 B.C. The biography of Apollonius of Tyana, written in 200 A.D., reports that when Apollonius arrived in Ephesus, "he found the people immersed in dissipation and cruel sports, in shows and panto-

Ephesus: First Century Stadium

mimes, and Pyrrhic dances, and all places resounded with song, and were filled with noise and debauchery." Although the famous Ephesian stadium near the gymnasium of Vedius was probably built in the reign of Nero (54-68 A.D.), a few years after St. Paul's stay in Ephesus, a smaller stadium built at the time of Lysimachus (ca. 355-281 B.C.) was already available. Here throngs roared their approval of foot racers, javelin throwers, relay teams, gladiators, and duels in which men fought lions, wolves and bears. Here, too, citizens may have flocked to

Ephesus: Relief of a Gladiator, on Marble Street

festivals honoring Artemis.

It is difficult to know whether or not to take St. Paul's reference to fighting beasts in Ephesus literally. That he was in danger is evident from his remark in his letter of introduction for Phoebe to the Ephesian Christians in which he included greetings to "Prisca and Aquila, my fellow workers in Christ Jesus, who risked their necks for my life, to whom not only I but also all the churches of the Gentiles give thanks." (Rom. 16:3-4).

A local Ephesian tradition identifies the large square tower near the port as the prison of St. Paul. The building is on the western end of Mount Coressus and was an integral part of the defensive wall built by Lysimachus in the 3rd century B.C. The hill is known as Astyagou Pagos after an inscription in the tower identifying the hill as the Hill of Astyages. We do not know who Astyages was. Recent archaeological and architectural studies have shown that the building could well have served as a prison. We do not know when the Ephesians began calling this building "St. Paul's prison," although it is mentioned in Western literature already by the 17th century Western travelers Thomas Smith, George Wheler, Jacques Spon, and Cornelius van Bruyn.

St. Paul's Prison Correspondence

LETTER TO THE PHILIPPIANS

In the early Church the existence of more than one letter by St. Paul to the Philippians was well known, for when Polycarp of Smyrna wrote the Philippians some eighty years later, he reminded them of the *letters* the Apostle had written them. What we know as the Letter to the Philippians is in fact two letters covering two separate situations.

St. Paul was able to receive visitors while in prison. When the church in Philippi learned that the Apostle was imprisoned, they raised money and sent one of their number, Epaphroditus,

to stay with St. Paul until the matter was settled. Ships sailed frequently from Macedonia to the Asian capital, and Epaphroditus easily was able to deliver the gift from the Philippians. St. Paul responded to this generosity in what some scholars consider his first letter to the Philippians (Phil. 3:2-4:23). Unfortunately, Epaphroditus fell sick while waiting on St. Paul, and when he recovered he returned to Philippi. Thereupon, St. Paul sent a letter, which is contained in Phil. 1:1-3:1, to protect Epaphroditus from being criticized for leaving while St. Paul was still a prisoner.

While in prison, the Apostle leaned heavily on the love and devotion of his brethren in the other churches, at the same time he recognized it as an unusual opportunity for the advance of the Gospel.

> I want you to know, brethren, that what has happened to me has really served to advance the gospel, so that it has become known throughout the whole praetorian guard and to all the rest that my imprisonment is for Christ; and most of the brethren have been made confident in the Lord because of my imprisonment, and are much more bold to speak the word of God without fear.
>
> Phil. 1:12-14

Though already put on trial (Phil 1:7, 16), the verdict had not been issued. St. Paul seemed to be convinced that he would be acquitted (Phil. 1:25), yet in spite of this hope and conviction, he still considered the possibility of condemnation (Phil. 2:17). The references to the "praetorian guard" and "those of Caesar's household" (Phil. 1:13, 4:22) indicate that he had come to know some of the soldiers stationed in the palace of the Roman governor. He shared with them his convictions and some of them had accepted the Christian faith.

Ephesus: The Traditional Prison of St. Paul

LETTER TO PHILEMON

While St. Paul was still in prison, together with Timothy and Epaphras, Onesimus, a young runaway slave, probably from Laodicea, came to the prison in Ephesus to see the Apostle. He had stolen from his master when he left and he hoped St. Paul somehow could free him from slavery. Onesimus's escape to Ephesus is the more plausible if we remember that the Temple of Artemis was a recognized place of refuge for thieves, debtors, and even murderers. Onesimus soon was won to the Christian faith.

Torn as he must have been, St. Paul realized his obligation to Onesimus's owners, Philemon, Apphia, and Archippus, prosperous Christians who had been converted by the Apostle when he had traveled through the cities of the Lycus Valley. St. Paul would have liked to keep Onesimus "in order that he might serve me on your behalf during my imprisonment for the gospel" (Philem. 13), although for all concerned it was necessary to send Onesimus back to the masters he had wronged. St. Paul sent with Onesimus a letter addressed to Philemon, Apphia, Archippus, and the church that met in their house commending Onesimus to them as a trustworthy Christian, and appealing to Philemon to forgive him and to receive him as a beloved brother. By returning, Onesimus could have been going to his death, for in the days of St. Paul owners could do what they liked to runaway slaves. Onesimus might have been tortured or thrown to wild beasts in the arena. Because St. Paul knew this, he wrote with authority to align the moral sentiment of the whole church in his appeal to Philemon. From St. Paul's Letter to the Colossians we infer that Onesimus returned to his master in company with Tychicus of Colossae (Col. 4:7-9). Apparently Philemon not only received Onesimus back but may even have freed him. Approximately sixty years later, Ignatius of Antioch wrote a letter from Smyrna to the church in Ephesus in which he spoke repeatedly about their bishop Onesimus. Of course, we cannot be sure that Onesimus, bishop of Ephesus ca. 107-117 A.D., was the runaway slave Onesimus whom the Apostle had returned to Philemon, but he may have been.

LETTER TO THE COLOSSIANS

Not much time could have elapsed between the arrival of Onesimus and the arrival of Epaphras, the leader of the church in Colossae. Colossae was one of the three Lycus Valley congregations together with Laodicea and Hierapolis. St. Paul might have visited the churches in Laodicea and Hierapolis although, apparently, he had only passed through Colossae, not meeting many people. He mentions his great concern "for those at Laodicea, and for all who have not seen my face" (Col. 2:1). Epaphras reported that his parishioners were deeply dissatisfied with the simplicity of the Pauline message, and that, therefore, they introduced more sophisticated cults consisting of various syncretic forms of their old philosophy and oriental beliefs and speculations. To them, Christ was one of many divine aeons, perhaps the greatest, but only one of many. This new teaching both threatened the belief in Christ's supremacy and created an esoteric group of Christians claiming superiority over the average Christians. They thought that physical matter was tainted with sin and, therefore, the incarnate Christ was inferior to angels. St. Paul answered the dissenting theologians in Colossae by exposing the heresy of their philosophy and stressing the adequacy of Christ. "Set your minds on things that are above, not on things that are on earth" (Col. 3:2).

Much concerned about the reception Onesimus would receive by the Christian brethren in the Lycus Valley, he included in his letter an admonition about their relationships with each other, known as "the household rules."

> Wives, be subject to your husbands, as is fitting in the Lord. Husbands, love your wives, and do not be harsh with them. Children, obey your parents in everything, for this pleases the Lord. Fathers, do not provoke your children, lest they become discouraged. Slaves, obey in everything those who are your earthly masters, not with eyeservice, as men-pleasers, but in singleness of heart, fearing the Lord. Whatever your task, work heartily, as

serving the Lord and not men, knowing that from the Lord you will receive the inheritance as your reward; you are serving the Lord Christ. For the wrongdoer will be paid back for the wrong he has done, and there is no partiality. Masters, treat your slaves justly and fairly, knowing that you also have a Master in heaven.

Col. 3:18-4:1

The issue of the relationship between slaves and their masters was still a very important matter to the Apostle, who dispatched this letter with Tychicus to Colossae (Col.4:7). The sending of Tychicus served an additional purpose, for he accompanied young Onesimus who was returning to Philemon.

St. Paul's situation in Ephesus must have deteriorated at the time he wrote the Colossians, for many of his loyal co-workers, on hearing of his plight, had assembled in the city of Diana. Together with St. Paul in prison was Aristarchus of the church in Thessalonica (Col. 4:10). Also in the city were Mark, the cousin of Barnabas, now reconciled to St. Paul; Jesus Justus; Epaphras, the minister to the Colossians; Luke, "the beloved physician;" and Demas. All of them were known to the Colossians at least by name, and they added their greetings to the letter.

The closing note included greetings to "Nympha and the church in her house" (Col. 4:15) and the instruction that "when this letter has been read among you, have it read also in the church of the Laodiceans; and see that you read also the letter from Laodicea" (Col. 4:16). We know nothing about this letter to the Laodiceans, unless we accept the view of some scholars that it was either St. Paul's Letter to Philemon or the Letter to the Ephesians.

In 60 A.D., a few years after St. Paul wrote this Letter to the Colossians, their city was destroyed by a severe earthquake. Although rebuilt, it never regained its former prominence. Most of the population of Colossae was Phrygian. The aristocracy was Greek and, according to Cicero, there was a large Jewish colony. In the beginning of the 9th century Colossae was destroyed and replaced by the new town of Chonae, the modern Honaz, a few miles to the south. The old name of the town was so completely forgotten that in the Middle Ages many people thought that the Colossians addressed by St. Paul were the inhabitants of the island Rhodes, because of their famous Colossus, one of the Seven Wonders of the ancient world!

LETTER TO THE CHURCHES OF ASIA

To the saints who are (at Ephesus) and faithful in Christ Jesus

Eph. 1:1.

This essay on St. Paul in Ephesus is not the place to repeat the lengthy and scholarly debates and arguments about the destination and authenticity of the Letter to the Ephesians. Two of the best and earliest Greek manuscripts, the Codex Sinaiticus and the Codex Vaticanus, omit the words "in Ephesus" from the first verse, and Origen of Alexandria (ca. 200 A.D.), the most scholarly investigator of the New Testament in the early Church, was hard pressed to explain the meaning of "to the saints who are..." In the middle of the 2nd century, Marcion gave to the letter the title "to the Laodiceans," obviously based on Col. 4:16, but also proving that his text mentioned no destination in Eph. 1:1.

The authorship of this letter, obviously an encyclical document, has been much disputed. Many scholars have assigned the letter to the post-Pauline period and ascribed it to one of the disciples of the Apostle as, for example, Onesimus of Ephesus. Assuming the letter was written by St. Paul, "a prisoner for Christ Jesus on behalf of you Gentiles" (Eph. 3:1), it was the last of the Apostle's prison letters. It was addressed to several or all of the churches in Asia. Tychicus, "the beloved brother and faithful minister in the Lord" (Eph. 6:21), who was sent to read the letter in the various churches, might have verbally inserted the appropriate name "in Ephesus," "in Laodicea," "in Hierapolis," wherever he went.

The Letter to the Ephesians is the most general of the Pauline letters and does not refer to any particular situation. The author speaks in several places about heresies undermining the unity of the Church, and thus the theme of the epistle has often been described as the "Unity and Divinity of the Church." As C.T. Wood said: "Like the Roman Empire with its many differing peoples and its varied modes of government adapted to each people, the Christian Church is composed of divers members, with their manifold traditions and temperamental gifts: but all are one in Christ, who sums them all up in Himself; the very diversity of the parts brings a richer life to the unity of the whole."

St. Paul and the Exorcists

Our ignorance of the timetable of the events described by the Apostle and St. Luke makes it virtually impossible for us to place them in chronological order. One of the stories recorded by St. Luke includes the Apostle's dealing with the exorcists of Ephesus.

And God did extraordinary miracles by the hands of Paul, so that handkerchiefs or aprons were carried away from his body to the sick, and diseases left them and the evil spirits came out of them. Then some of the itinerant Jewish exorcists undertook to pronounce the name of the Lord Jesus over those who had evil spirits, saying, "I adjure you by the Jesus whom Paul preaches." Seven sons of a Jewish high priest named Sceva were doing this. But the evil spirit answered them, "Jesus I know, and Paul I know; but who are you?" And the man in whom the evil spirit was leaped on them, mastered all of them, and overpowered them, so that they fled out of that house naked and wounded. And this became known to all residents of Ephesus, both Jews and Greeks; and fear fell upon them all; and the name of the Lord Jesus was extolled. Many also of those who were now believers came, confessing and divulging their practices. And a number of those who practiced magic arts brought their books together and burned them in the sight of all; and they counted the value of them and found it came to fifty thousand pieces of silver. So the word of the Lord grew and prevailed mightily.

Acts 19:11-20

For two years St. Paul taught in the hall of Tyrannus. He had ministered to the Jews and Gentiles in Ephesus, and was instrumental in spreading the Gospel throughout the province of Asia. He was imprisoned for his beliefs. He had comforted, counseled, and strengthened those in distress. In short, he had become well known in Ephesus and throughout the province of Asia.

St. Paul's miraculous powers also were well known. In his II Corinthians 12:12, St. Paul reminded the Corinthians of the miracles he had wrought among them by saying, "the signs of a true apostle were performed among you in all patience, with signs and wonders and mighty works."

In Lystra he had healed a cripple (Acts 14:8-10), in Philippi he exorcised a slave girl with a spirit of divination (Acts 16:16-18), in Melite he healed the father of Publius, the chief man of the island, of a fever and dysentery (Acts 28:7-8). He continued these practices in Ephesus, to the extent that the faithful touched their handkerchiefs or aprons to the Apostle and then carried them to the sick. Like the fringe of Christ's garment (Matthew 9:20, 14:36) or St. Peter's shadow (Acts 5:12-16), St. Paul's clothes were superstitiously credited with miraculous healing power.

Ephesus was well known among the cities of the eastern Roman world as a center for the study and practice of magic. Perhaps even more than Pisidian Antioch, Corinth, and Antioch-on-the-Orontes, this city of traders and sailors, of courtesans and rakes, swarmed with soothsayers and purveyors of charms. In the *Life of Apollonius of Tyana* by Philostratus (170-245 A.D.) there is a passage describing the Ephesians, "They were devoted to dancers and taken up with pantomines, and the whole city was full of pipers, and full of effeminate rascals, and full of noise." When the Temple of Artemis was burned, the magi of Ephesus prophesied that "the great scourge and destroyer of Asia," meaning Alexander the Great, was born the same day. The importance of cults in Ephesus was so great in the latter part of the 1st century that the emperor Vespasian maintained a celebrated astrologer named Balbillus in Ephesus although he had banished all magicians and astrologers from Rome.

Exorcising spirits in the name of Jesus was widely practised in the early Church, but the attempt by itinerant Jewish exorcists to do so in the name of "Jesus whom Paul preaches" was clearly usurpation of authority. Their attempt did not succeed, however, and they themselves were overpowered by the evil spirit they sought to control. The point of this story was intended for all Christians; that healings and exorcisms depended as much upon the integrity of the healer as upon the faith of the afflicted.

As a result of this incident, some Ephesian practitioners of magic were converted to Christianity. They collected their books on magic, valued at least at $10,000 and burned them publicly. Among these books were probably some of the so-called Ephesian Letters, charms which were believed to make their bearers invincible. A wrestler wearing them would be victorious thirty times, but he would be defeated immediately if they were discovered or removed by his opponent. Croesus is said to have escaped being burned alive by having pronounced them on the pyre, and magicians used to exorcise demons by having people possessed by demons recite the Ephesian Letters. There were six of them, and Clement of Alexandria interpreted them as standing for darkness, light, earth, the four seasons of the year, the sun, and truth.

The conversion of the exorcists and their followers was enough of a success that the Apostle felt able to leave Ephesus for Macedonia and Achaia.

> Now after these events Paul resolved in the Spirit to pass through Macedonia and Achaia and go to Jerusalem, saying, "After I have been there, I must also see Rome." And having sent into Macedonia two of his helpers, Timo-

thy and Erastus, he himself stayed in Asia for a while.

Acts 19:21-22

That St. Paul wanted to revisit the churches in Macedonia and Achaia is confirmed by his own writings. To the Corinthians he wrote "I wanted to visit you on my way to Macedonia, and to come back to you from Macedonia and have you send me on my way to Judea" (II Cor. 1:16). We do not know what made Paul change his plans, but instead "he stayed in Asia for a while" (Acts 19:22), in Ephesus, where the silversmiths' riot, one of the most vividly described episodes of the Apostle's ministry, occurred.

The Silversmiths' Riot

About that time there arose no little stir concerning the Way. For a man named Demetrius, a silversmith, who made silver shrines of Artemis, brought no little business to the craftsmen. These he gathered together, with the workmen of like occupation, and said, "Men, you know that from this business we have our wealth. And you see and hear that not only at Ephesus but almost throughout all Asia this Paul has persuaded and turned away a considerable company of people, saying that gods made with hands are not gods. And there is danger not only that this trade of ours may come into disrepute but also that the temple of the great goddess Artemis may count for nothing, and that she may even be deposed from her magnificence, she whom all Asia and the world worship."

When they heard this they were enraged, and cried out, "Great is Artemis of the Ephesians!" So the city was filled with the confusion; and they rushed together into the theater, dragging with them Gaius and Aristarchus, Macedonians who were Paul's companions in travel. Paul

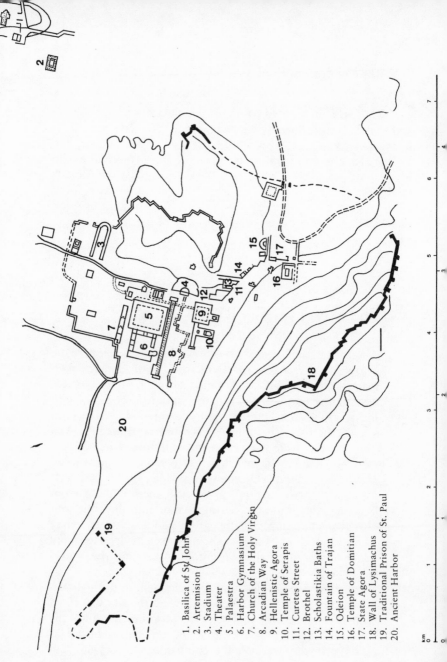

1. Basilica of St. John
2. Artemision
3. Stadium
4. Theater
5. Palaestra
6. Harbor Gymnasium
7. Church of the Holy Virgin
8. Arcadian Way
9. Hellenistic Agora
10. Temple of Serapis
11. Curetes Street
12. Brothel
13. Scholastikia Baths
14. Fountain of Trajan
15. Odeion
16. Temple of Domitian
17. State Agora
18. Wall of Lysimachus
19. Traditional Prison of St. Paul
20. Ancient Harbor

wished to go in among the crowd, but the disciples would not let him; some of the Asiarchs also, who were friends of his, sent to him and begged him not to venture into the theater. Now some cried one thing, some another; for the assembly was in confusion, and most of them did not know why they had come together. Some of the crowd prompted Alexander, whom the Jews had put forward. And Alexander motioned with his hand, wishing to make a defense to the people. But when they recognized that he was a Jew, for about two hours they all with one voice cried out, "Great is Artemis of the Ephesians!" And when the town clerk had quieted the crowd, he said, "Men of Ephesus, what man is there who does not know that the city of the Ephesians is temple keeper of the great Artemis, and of the sacred stone that fell from the sky? Seeing then that these things cannot be contradicted, you ought to be quiet and do nothing rash. For you have brought these men here who are neither sacrilegious nor blasphemers of our goddess. If therefore Demetrius and the craftsmen with him have a complaint against any one, the courts are open, and there are proconsuls; let them bring charges against one another. But if you seek anything further, it shall be settled in the regular assembly. For we are in danger of being charged with rioting today, there being no cause that we can give to justify this commotion." And when he had said this, he dismissed the assembly. After the uproar ceased, Paul sent for the disciples and having exhorted them took leave of them and departed for Macedonia.

Acts 19:23 - 20:1

St. Paul had planned to stay in Ephesus until the feast of Pentecost "for a wide door for effective work" (I Cor. 16:9) had opened to him. Some scholars think that "the wide door"

Hellenistic - Roman Ephesus

was occasioned by the Artemisia, or Ephesia, the annual festival held in honor of Artemis. The festival provided a splendid opportunity to do missionary work, for during it the city was crowded with people from all over Asia Minor. The festival was held during the month of Artemision which fell sometime in April or May.

The scene of the silversmiths' riot was the famous Ephesian theater, one of the largest in the province of Asia, with a capacity of almost 25,000 spectators. It was in the center of the city at the intersection of Marble Street and the Arcadian Way on the western slopes of Mount Pion. Its construction had been started under the emperor Claudius (34-41 A.D.), but it was not completed until the days of Trajan (98-117 A.D.). To picture the silversmiths' riot, therefore, we should envisage the building covered with scaffolding and the laborers watching the unexpected event. The theater also served as the regular place for the citizens' assembly, which was held three times a month. These meetings were chaired by the town clerk, one of the most important political figures in the city.

St. Paul's preaching was threatening the trade in silver shrines of Artemis. As Professor G.H.C. Macgregor said: "When devotion to religion and patriotic sentiment can be made to coincide with self-interest, then fanatical intolerance knows no bounds!" No silver models of the Temple of Artemis have been discovered, although shrines of terra cotta and marble have been excavated. An inscription, dated to 104 A.D., found on one of the walls of the southern passage into the theater, describes in detail a single offering from a man named Vibius Salutaris. This offering consisted of 29 images probably similar to those made by Demetrius and his fellow craftsmen. Made of gold and silver and weighing from three to seven pounds each, they were figures of Artemis with two stags and a variety of symbolic figures. These objects were dedicated to Artemis, carried in public processions throughout Ephesus, and then placed in her temple.

Diana of Ephesus, 1st. Century A.D.

In Ephesus, Artemis was not the virginal deity of the wild who roamed through the mountains and forests with her nymphs. Artemis of Ephesus was a goddess of fertility, a form of the great Asiatic mother goddess. She was represented from neck to waist covered with a large number of breasts in the form of small eggs. Her legs were fused together and made the statue resemble a pillar. Demetrius's claim that Artemis of Ephesus was worshipped throughout Asia and the world (Acts 19:27) was supported by the large number of pilgrims who attended the Artemisia. The statue of the goddess in the temple was believed to be of supernatural origin, that it had fallen from the sky (Acts 19:35). St. Paul had preached "that gods made with hands are not gods" (Acts 19:26), a charge to which the town clerk responded when he pointed out that the statue of this goddess had not been made by human hands. Among the stones lining Curetes Street, about thirty yards below the Temple of Hadrian and lying flat behind the upright row, is a statue base erected by the college of silversmiths, the same to which Demetrius probably belonged.

After Demetrius had called together the members of the guild and spoken to them about the economic consequences of St. Paul's teaching, they angrily rushed forth into the street. Their momentum pulled other people with them into the theater. Most of the crowd was ignorant of the specific cause of the tumult, knowing only that the issue concerned the city goddess. On their way to the theater the crowd seized two of the Apostle's companions, Gaius and Aristarchus. Gaius was from Derbe in Galatia and Aristarchus was from Thessalonica (Acts 20:4). The Jews put forward a man named Alexander to address the mob, probably because they feared that the crowd might turn against them for their own hostility to idolatry. It has been suggested that this Alexander may have been the coppersmith named Alexander who afterwards did Paul great harm (II Tim. 4:14). Whoever he was, the crowd refused to hear him, and for about two hours shouted "Great is Artemis of the Ephesians!" The noise must have been tremendous, for the acoustics of the theater are excellent even today, and at that time were even better because of bronze and clay sounding vessels placed throughout the auditorium.

The town clerk finally managed to calm the crowd. He told the people that the supremacy of Artemis was not in peril, that the Christians had neither robbed the temple nor blasphemed the goddess, and that for any complaints and disputes the courts were available. He also pointed out that the real danger was not the loss of their trade but rather "of being charged with rioting," for which the Roman authorities might punish the city.

St. Paul wished to go in among the crowd to defend himself, but was prevented from doing so by the disciples and "some of the Asiarchs also, who were friends of his." Asiarchs were provincial officials responsible for the politico-religious organisation of Asia in the worship of Rome and the emperors. They were in charge of the festivals and games, and while they were priests from a religious point of view, they were also officers of the imperial service. One of the titles of the reigning Asiarch was High Priest of Asia. St. Luke's reference to the representatives of the official Roman cult as friends of St. Paul is an important point. In his account of St. Paul's stay in Ephesus he had omitted Paul's imprisonment by the Roman authorities and ignored Paul's sufferings. He sought to show that his hero moved within the confines of Roman law and that the new faith was compatible with the Roman Empire. Just as the town clerk's speech reads like an *apologia* for the Christian message, so the reference to the Asiarchs as friends of the Apostle is another indication that St. Paul's troubles were the result of popular hostility, against which he was protected by friendly Roman officials.

The Asiarchs probably suggested that St. Paul should leave the city to avoid future disturbances. After meeting once more with his disciples and embracing them, he took a coastal vessel to Troy and then sailed on to Macedonia.

St. Paul's Letter to the Ephesians

The document known as the Letter to the Ephesians was in fact not written to the Ephesians but to all the churches in Asia. Nevertheless, we do possess a letter to the Ephesian church, which is contained in St. Paul's Letter to the Romans 16:1-24. The full textual argument for this statement is detailed, but these twenty-four verses cannot be considered as part of the Epistle to the Romans. For one thing, the text indicates extensive personal knowledge of the congregation, and at the time it was written St. Paul had not yet been to Rome. Instead, these verses are a letter of recommendation for Phoebe, a deaconess of the church of Cenchreae, the eastern harbor of Corinth. She was about to journey to Ephesus.

The letter was dictated by the Apostle during his final visit to Corinth, when he stayed in the home of Gaius (Rom. 16:23). Phoebe was going to the city where the Apostle had just spent three years, and it was only natural that he should use the opportunity to send greetings to his many friends in Ephesus and thereby introduce Phoebe to them. This is a most welcome document for it throws interesting light upon the Christian community in Ephesus. There are Priscilla and Aquila, who had "risked their necks" for the Apostle, and who were hosts to one of the Ephesian house churches (Rom. 16:3-4). A special greeting is extended to the "beloved Epaenetus, who was the first convert in Asia for Christ" (Rom. 16:5). Andronicus and Junias, who had been fellow prisoners with St. Paul are referred to as "kinsmen" and "men of note among the apostles" (Rom. 16:7). They had accepted the Christian faith before St. Paul, and perhaps had been converted by St. John. Ampliatus is the Apostle's "beloved in the Lord" (Rom. 16:8) and Urbanus is his "fellow worker in Christ" (Rom. 16:9). Then there is his beloved Stachys" (Rom. 16:9), who may have been the leader of the house church in Hierapolis, where Philip proclaimed the Gospel. We do not know if Aristobulus, to whose family greetings are sent, was the Aristobulus who was said to be the brother of the Apostle Barnabas. In addition to the house church of Priscilla and Aquila, greetings are also sent to "Asyncritus, Phlegon, Hermes, Patrobas, Hermas and the brethren who are with them" (Rom. 16:14) and to "Philologus, Julia, Nerens and his sister, and Olympus, and all the saints who are with them" (Rom. 16:15). A special greeting is extended to "Rufus, eminent in the Lord, also his mother and mine" (Rom. 16:13). Was he perhaps the son of Simon of Cyrene mentioned in Mark 15:21? We are told that Simon, who was forced to bear the cross of Jesus to Golgotha, was the father of Alexander and Rufus. The statement that Rufus's mother was also a mother to the Apostle suggests an intimate acquaintance. This long list of twenty-six names indicates a familiarity with a Christian community which St. Paul could have gained only during his long and intense ministry in Ephesus.

As in his two letters to the Corinthians and his letter to the Thessalonians, St. Paul reminds his converts to "greet one another with a holy kiss" (Rom. 16:16). The warning against "those who create dissensions and difficulties" are the words of a pastor to a congregation threatened by heretical teachings. To his final greetings are joined those of Timothy, Lucius of Cyrene (Acts 13:1), Jason of Thessalonica (Acts 17:5-9), Sosipater of Beroea (Acts 20:4) and Erastus the city treasurer. The last was an important person in Corinth. Among the most interesting discoveries in Corinth is an inscribed block used in an ancient repair of a pavement in the little square at the northern end of the street leading past the theater. The letters are deeply hollowed out and read

ERASTVS PRO AEDILITATE
S P STRAVIT
(ERASTVS PRO AEDILITATE SUA PECUNIA STRAVIT)

"Erastus, in return for his aedilship, laid the pavement at his own expense." St. Paul's Letter to the Ephesians concludes with a blessing "the grace of our Lord Jesus Christ be with you all. Amen" (Rom. 16:24).

St. Paul's Message to the Elders of Ephesus

And from Miletus he sent to Ephesus and called to him the elders of the church. And when they came to him, he said to them:

"You yourselves know how I lived among you all the time from the first day that I set foot in Asia, serving the Lord with all humility and with tears and with trials which befell me through the plots of the Jews; how I did not shrink from declaring to you anything that was profitable, and teaching you in public and from house to house, testifying both to Jews and to Greeks of repentance to God and of faith in our Lord Jesus Christ. And now, behold, I am going to Jerusalem, bound in the Spirit, not knowing what shall befall me there; except that the Holy Spirit testifies to me in every city that imprisonment and afflictions await me. But I do not account my life of any value nor as precious to myself, if only I may accomplish my course and the ministry which I received from the Lord Jesus, to testify to the gospel of the grace of God. And now, behold, I know that all you among whom I have gone about preaching the kingdom will see my face no more. Therefore I testify to you this day that I am innocent of the blood of all of you, for I did not shrink from declaring to you the whole counsel of God. Take heed to yourselves and to all the flock, in which the Holy Spirit has made you guardians, to feed the church of the Lord which he obtained for himself with his own blood. I know that after my departure fierce wolves will come in among you, not sparing the flock; and from among your own selves will arise men speaking perverse things, to draw away the disciples after them. Therefore be alert, remembering that for three years I did not cease night or day to admonish every one with tears. And now I commend you to God and to the word of his grace, which is able to build you up and to give you the inheritance among all those who are consecrated. I coveted no one's silver or gold or apparel. You yourselves know that these hands ministered to my necessities, and to those who were with me. In all things I have shown you that by so toiling one must help the weak, remembering the words of the Lord Jesus, how he said, It is more blessed to give than to receive.' "

And when he had spoken thus, he knelt down and prayed with them all. And they all wept and embraced Paul and kissed him, sorrowing most of all because of the word he had spoken, that they should see his face no more. And they brought him to the ship.

Acts 20:17-38

According to Sir William M. Ramsay's chronology of the travels of St. Paul, the Apostle arrived at Miletus early on

Miletus: The River God Meander, in the Baths of Faustina

Thursday, 28 April 57. Miletus, famous for its market gate now in the Pergamum Museum in Berlin, was the birthplace of such notable men as Thales, one of the seven wise men, his student Anaximander, and Anaximander's student Anaximenes. Strabo informs us that Miletus had four harbors, of which one could hold an entire fleet. The ship carrying the Apostle would have docked in the lion's bay, named after the lion monuments near the port. To the west of the smaller Grattius monument was the synagogue of Miletus. The existence of a Jewish congregation in this port city is also attested by an inscription in one of the steps of the large theater. We do not know the origin of the Christian community in Miletus. Did St. Paul proclaim the Gospel to the Miletans during his stay in Ephesus? Did people from Miletus attend some of the services the Apostle conducted in Ephesus?

St. Paul avoided Ephesus because he was in a hurry to reach Jerusalem, and had he gone to Ephesus he would have become involved with his many friends and their problems. He also may have wanted to avoid the risk of meeting his enemies. No doubt he was also running something of a risk in Miletus, for that city had a large Jewish community which may have been hostile to him. He invited the Ephesian elders to a quiet spot on the outskirts of the city for the meeting, which is one of the most touching episodes in the Acts of the Apostles. He reminded the elders of the opposition of the Ephesian Jews which had caused him tears, trials, and imprisonment. Now he was on his way to Jerusalem expecting more affliction, which he saw as a culmination of his ministry. He was deeply concerned about heretics and schismatics in Ephesus, and he admonished the elders to remain alert, commending them to God. The elders wept that they would not see the Apostle again. They accompanied him to the ship which carried him via the islands of Cos and Rhodes to Patara from where he sailed to Tyre and then on to Caesarea.

Miletus: The Delphinion

The Ephesian Collection of St. Paul's Letters

Prof. Edgar J. Goodspeed suggested that towards the end of the 1st century one of St. Paul's Ephesian disciples collected St. Paul's letters and the fragments of his letters, and edited and arranged them into a corpus of Pauline literature. Such a collection was not a new idea, for the practice of assembling the published letters of distinguished persons was widespread in the Graeco-Roman world, as seen by the collections of letters of Plato, Aristotle, and Epicurus. The collection of Cicero's letters became our most reliable source of information about life in Rome in the first century B.C. Other letter collections included those of St. Paul's contemporary, Apollonius of Tyana, while Pliny published his own letters, which he dedicated to his friend Septicius.

The nucleus of St. Paul's collection of letters consisted probably of his letters to the Colossians and Philemon, both of which were easily available in Ephesus. Some of the other documents must have been more difficult to obtain, but the central location of Ephesus facilitated easy communication with the churches in Galatia, Macedonia, Achaia, and Rome, which had received Pauline letters. The collector has remained anonymous, though it has been suggested that Onesimus of Ephesus may have assembled the Pauline corpus, especially since he was already familiar with St. Paul's letters to the Colossians and to Philemon. Is it only coincidence that about the same time these Pauline letters were collected, John, the Seer of Patmos, introduced his Revelation with a corpus of seven letters addressed to the churches of Asia? The writer of these letters clearly was familiar with most of the Pauline letters. Some years later, other Christian letters were assembled in Asia, for example, the seven letters by St. Ignatius, and the three letters by John the Elder. Ephesus was the home of John, the Seer of Patmos, before he was imprisoned on that island, and also the place in which the Gospel of St. John was written. The city had become the outstanding Christian literary center of the 1st century. This must in large part be because of the collection of the Pauline literature, which left a lasting mark upon such documents as the Letter to the Hebrews, I Clement, I Peter, and the letters of St. Ignatius and St. Polycarp.

EARLY AND MEDIEVAL
CHRISTIANITY IN EPHESUS

By the second half of the 1st century Ephesus had become the main center for the propagation of the Gospel among the Gentiles and the Hellenistic Jews of the Roman Empire. It is only natural, therefore, that stories of Christian personalities should have become attached to this city and help make it a major pilgrimage site. The importance of Ephesus in the early and medieval Christian church can be shown by the reports of two typical pilgrims. In 1106-7 the Russian abbot Daniel visited the tomb of St. John and related that a holy dust, which was gathered by believers as a cure for diseases, arose from the tomb on the anniversary of St. John's death. Daniel also visited the relics of the three hundred fathers and of St. Alexander, the cave of the Seven Sleepers, the tomb of St. Mary Magdalene, and the tomb of the Apostle Timothy. He saw the image of the Holy Virgin, which at that time was believed to have been used at the Council of Ephesus to refute Nestorius. In 1304 Ramon Mantaner-Buchon reported miracles at the tomb of St. John and wrote that the exudations of the tomb were beneficial for childbirth, fever, and would calm the stormy sea. The Turks found relics of St. John to be valuable items for trade. A piece of the True Cross taken by St. John to Ephesus, a cloth made by Mary and given to St. John, and a copy of the Revelation to John written in gold by St. John himself they exchanged for grain with Ticino Zacario, one of the Latin princes of western Asia Minor.

Selçuk: The Basilica of St. John

St. John in Ephesus

Any discussion of St. John in Ephesus is complicated because of the problem of identity. Some people maintain that there is only one person who is known as: John the brother of James, John the son of Zebedee and Salome, the beloved disciple, the Apostle John, John the Theologian, John the Evangelist, John the Elder, John the Seer of Patmos. Early Christian tradition, however, identified at least two men named John. Modern scholarsip, on the other hand, has suggested that there were even three prominent early Christian figures named John. This is not the place, however, to elaborate on this thorny issue and we shall distinguish only between St. John the Apostle and St. John the Seer of Patmos.

St. John the Apostle in Ephesus

The tradition that the Apostle John came to Ephesus was widely believed by the early Church and still has supporters today. The Apostle John was the son of Zebedee and Salome, the brother of James, and the beloved disciple of Jesus Christ. There is no agreement among the church fathers or among modern scholars concerning the date of his sojourn in Ephesus. He was a Galilean fisherman, and had followed the call of Jesus and became a member of the inner circle of the apostles, witnessing among other things the transfiguration of his Lord. After the resurrection, he gave the right hand of fellowship to Paul and Barnabas, indicating that they should go to the Gentiles while he, James, and Peter should turn to the circumcised (Gal. 2:9). The Apostle John was in Jerusalem in 46 A.D., at the time of St. Paul's second visit to the city. The later history of his life falls into the realm of tradition. According to a statement attributed to Papias, the bishop of Hierapolis in the first half of the 2nd century, and supported also by other evidence, the Apostle John, as his brother St. James, was killed by the Jews before the year 70 A.D.

A Syriac fragment appended to the Armenian translation of St. Ephrem's commentary on Tatian's *Diatessaron* states that "John wrote the gospel in Greek in Antioch, for he remained in the country until the time of Trajan." On the other hand, Tertullian (150-230 A.D.) mentioned that the Apostle John came to Asia early. Polycrates, the 2nd century bishop of Ephesus, writing to Victor, bishop of Rome, stated, "moreover, John, that rested on the bosom of our Lord, who was a priest that bore the sacerdotal plate, and martyr and teacher, he also rests at Ephesus."

St. Irenaeus, a disciple of Polycarp of Smyrna, who was in turn a disciple of the Apostle John, stated that John wrote his gospel while living at Ephesus. The 4th century church historian Eusebius repeats the apostolic tradition, according to which "the disciples of our Saviour, being scattered over the whole world... John received Asia, where after continuing for some time, he died at Ephesus." According to St. Jerome (340-420), John established and governed all the churches in Asia and died in Ephesus.

Whereas tradition has consistently identified the author of the Fourth Gospel and the three Johannine letters with the Apostle John, modern scholarship maintains that these documents were written by an anonymous author, known as John the Elder (II John 1:1, III John 1:1) who also lived in Ephesus.

In the 2nd century a small church was built to enshrine the tomb of St. John. In the 4th century it was enlarged into the so-called Theodosian basilica. In the 6th century the famous Justinian basilica of St. John, one of the most magnificent churches of early Christianity, was built on the same site. It is in the town of Selçuk, a little more than two miles northeast of the Graeco-Roman settlement of Ephesus. The church surmounts the hill known as Ayasoluk after the former name of the town, Haghios Theologos, i.e. the Apostle John, "the theologian." This large basilica, 360 feet long and 130 feet wide, attracted large numbers of pilgrims throughout the centuries. In the Middle Ages, pilgrims from the West traveled to Ephesus to behold the site blessed by the Apostle John. In 1102 the pilgrim Saewulf crossed from Patmos to Ephesus where the Apostle John "entered the sepulchre living," and Sir Maundeville in the account of his journey in 1322 writes that "from Patmos men go to Ephesus, a fair city and nigh to the sea. And there died St. John, and was buried in a tomb behind the high altar. And there is a fair church, for the Christians were always wont to hold the place."

This monumental church had three naves separated by two rows of massive pillars faced with white marble. The other walls and the elaborate superstructures were built of brick. At the east of the church was a large semicircular apse which had a raised floor. Below the altar room was a crypt with several rooms, including the tomb of St. John. When the crypt was excavated in 1928 no relics of St. John were found.

St. John, the Seer of Patmos, in Ephesus

Eusebius, the 4th century bishop of Caesarea in Palestine, quoting the 2nd century bishop Papias, mentioned the existence of two disciples named John who worked in Asia. "The statement of those is true, who assert there were two of the same name in Asia, that there were also two tombs in Ephesus, and that both are called John's even to this day; which it is particularly necessary to observe. For it is probable that the second, if it be not allowed that it was the first, saw the Revelation ascribed to John."

John of Patmos is the seer who refers to himself as "I John, your brother, who share with you in Jesus the tribulation and the kingdom and the patient endurance, was on the island called Patmos on account of the word of God and the testimony of Jesus" (Rev. 1:9). Several scholars have pointed out that John, who wrote the Revelation during the persecutions of Domitian ca. 95 A.D., had lived in Ephesus where he had become familiar with the Ephesian collection of St. Paul's letters. This collection of Pauline letters had become so popular that John may have taken it as a model for his introduction to Revelation (Rev. 2:1-3:22).

We know very little about this John. He calls himself a brother of the Christians he addressed. He had testified to the Christian faith in Ephesus and consequently was exiled by Domitian to the island of Patmos. He probably had refused to worship the image of the emperor, a test that was often applied to Christians. It is assumed that John returned from exile to Ephesus during the lenient reign of Nerva, the successor of Domitian, where he died and was buried.

The Holy Virgin Mary in Ephesus

The tradition of the sojourn and dormition of the Holy Virgin in Ephesus is based on the assumption that the Apostle John, together with St. Mary, departed from Jerusalem for Asia soon after the ascension of Jesus Christ. The Gospel according to John records that on the Cross Jesus Christ commissioned the Apostle John to take responsibility for His mother.

> When Jesus saw his mother, and the disciple whom he loved standing near, he said to his mother, "Woman, behold, your son!" Then he said to the disciple, "Behold, your mother!" And from that hour the disciple took her to his own home.
>
> John 19:26, 27

Some scholars have maintained that the phrase "to his own home" should mean "his home in Ephesus," since this was the city of his missionary activities. St. Luke, who has provided us with much information about the Holy Virgin, omitted any mention in his Acts of the Apostles about the Holy Virgin's life after her presence at the occasion of the ascension of her Son from the Mount of Olives. But the argument that the Scriptures are silent about St. Mary in Ephesus should not necessarily be used against the possible sojourn of the Holy Virgin in the city of Diana, for we have seen that St. Luke omitted many incidents in the life of St. Paul, such as the Ephesian imprisonment, from his

113

account. One of the earliest references to the Holy Virgin's travels to Asia is found in St. Epiphanius's (315-402 A.D.) *Panarion*, where it is stated that "while John meanwhile left for Asia, nothing is said that he took the Holy Virgin with him as a companion on the journey, concerning this matter scripture is utterly silent." This statement by the bishop of Salamis in Cyprus presupposes the circulation of a tradition of St. Mary's travel to Asia, for which he found no Scriptural authority. In 431 A.D. the Third Ecumenical Council, convoked in Ephesus, produced a letter condemning the Nestorians as heretics, and mentioned that Nestorius himself was present in Ephesus "in which place (were) John the Theologian and the Holy Virgin Mary, Mother of God." In the Middle Ages a tradition existed that "the Apostle John passed a great part of his life at Ephesus, and died there; as did the Virgin Mary."

Father Bernard F. Deutsch, who investigated the pertinent references of the Holy Virgin's sojourn and dormition at Ephesus, cited two particular traditions, a Syrian Jacobite tradition and one maintained by the people of Kirkindje, a village in the hills east of Ephesus. The tradition is first recorded by Moses bar Kepha, a 9th century Syrian bishop and theologian: "St. John took the Virgin Mary with him when he left Jerusalem for Asia Minor and they settled in Ephesus where the Virgin Mary died, and her tomb is in Ephesus." Three hundred years later, Michael the Syrian, a Jacobite patriarch of Antioch, wrote in his *Chronicle*: "John preached at Antioch and afterwards went to Ephesus and the Mother of Our Lord accompanied him. Soon afterwards, they were exiled to the isle of Patmos. On returning from exile, he preached at Ephesus and built a church. Ignatius and Polycarp assisted him; he buried the blessed Mary. He lived 73 years and died after all the apostles; he was buried at Ephesus." Gregory Abu'l-Faraj, known as Bar Hebraeus, the last of the great Jacobite writers (1226-1286), added to this statement that St. John buried the Holy Virgin at Ephesus but kept the exact place secret. These medieval Syrian references are in interesting contrast to the Orthodox tradition that the tomb of the Holy Virgin is in the Valley of Jehosaphat outside the walls of Jerusalem.

114

Until the latter part of the 19th century, Orthodox Christians of the village of Kirkindje joined an annual pilgrimage on the Feast of the Assumption (August 15) to Panaya Kapula on the Bulbul Dagh, where they celebrated the Divine Liturgy. The name Panaya Kapula is a hybrid of Greek and Turkish meaning the house of the All Holy, i.e., the Virgin. The Christians of Kirkindje were said to be descendants of Ephesian Christians who were driven from Ephesus in the 11th century. In 1922 the Christians of this village left and the name was changed to Serindje. The Kirkindje Christians had retained a tradition which would have died when they left the area had it not been for the visions of the Augustinian nun, Anne Catherine Emmerich, which revived interest in the Holy Virgin's sojourn in the city.

Catherine Emmerich (1774-1824), born in Goesfeld, Germany, to a peasant family, experienced visions from her early youth. At the age of 37 she began to bear the stigmata of Christ's passion on her own body and to have ecstatic visions. Many of her visions were transcribed by the prominent romanticist Clemens Maria Brentano who, ten years after Catherine Emmerich's death, published those pertaining to Christ under the title *The Dolorous Passion of Our Lord.* In 1821 and 1822, at about the time of the Feast of the Assumption, Catherine Emmerich had described the Holy Virgin's sojourn in Ephesus, a city the nun had never visited for she lived all her life in Germany.

> After Our Lord's ascension Mary lived for three years on Mount Sion, for three years in Bethany, and for nine years in Ephesus, whither St. John took her... Mary did not live in Ephesus itself ... her dwelling was on a hill to the left of the road from Jerusalem some three and a half hours from Ephesus... It was on this plateau that the Jewish settlers had made their home ... John had a house built for the Holy Virgin before he brought her here... Mary's house was the only one built of stone. A little way behind it was the summit of the rocky hill from which one could see over the trees and hills to Ephesus and the sea with its many islands.

The topographical details were remarkably accurate, but also the description of the house in which the Holy Virgin was believed to have resided provided minute details as to the location of her bedroom, the fireplace, and the position of the windows.

In July 1891 Father Eugene Poulin, superior of the Lazarist College in Smyrna, together with three other persons, went to Ephesus to verify the description of the "House of Mary" as given by Catherine Emmerich. On the site mentioned, the Lazarists found the ruins of an ancient house which had been transformed into a chapel. After all, the nun had said that "the apostles had made St. Mary's room in the house into a church." In 1892 an inquiry was held on the site by Msgr. André Timoni, Archbishop of Smyrna and Vicar Apostolic of Asia Minor, and eventually pilgrimages to Panaya Kapulu were authorized. Archaeologists have dated the ruins from the 1st to the 16th century. Most of the remains are dated to the 6th century, while there are some sections of the walls which may date to the 1st century A.D. The tradition of the sojourn of the Holy Virgin in Ephesus is one of the gems of Christian piety and devotion which has led many pilgrims to a deeper appreciation of the Christian faith. Where once pilgrims from all over the ancient world assembled to offer their devotion to Diana, there the cult to the goddess was replaced by the veneration of the Holy Virgin Mary.

Mary Magdalene in Ephesus

The tradition of Mary Magdalene's sojourn and death in

Ephesus: Panaya Kapulu

Ephesus can be traced to the 6th century. Gregory of Tours (538-594 A.D.) wrote that "in Ephesus is found the place where this apostle (John) wrote the Gospel... in that city Mary Magdalene rests." Mary Magdalene is first mentioned by St. Luke as one of the women who had been healed of evil spirits and infirmities. She accompanied Jesus Christ on His last journey to Jerusalem, witnessed the crucifixion and the burial. Her encounter with the Risen Christ is beautifully portrayed in John 20: 1-18.

Tradition does not inform us about Mary Magdalene's journey to Ephesus, although we may assume that the church fathers believed she traveled together with John and the Holy Virgin. Throughout the Middle Ages the belief in St. Mary Magdalene's sojourn was faithfully maintained. A tomb, believed to be that of St. Mary Magdalene, was discovered in 1952 by the French archaeologist, Louis Massignon, at the entrance to the Grotto of the Seven Sleepers of Ephesus.

St. Timothy in Ephesus

Timothy of Lystra was a loyal associate of St. Paul on his missionary journeys in Macedonia and Achaia. From Corinth he accompanied the Apostle to Ephesus where he was imprisoned with him. According to I Tim. 1:3 St. Paul left Timothy in Ephesus to "charge certain persons not to teach any different doctrine." Eusebius Pamphylus stated "that Timothy is recorded as having first received the episcopate at Ephesus." During the reign of Domitian he is said to have suffered martyrdom by being clubbed to death for protesting against the orgies associated with the cult of Artemis. The martyrium of St. Timothy, first mentioned in the 6th century, was venerated in Ephesus on Mount Pion, although the relics of the bishop were translated to Constantinople in 356 A.D.

St. Luke in Ephesus

The evangelist and author of Acts met St. Paul in either Antioch or Philippi and joined him on his missionary journeys. During St. Paul's imprisonment in Ephesus, St. Luke the "beloved physician," shared the Apostle's trials and tribulations. After the Apostle's departure, St. Luke joined him on his further travels. An ancient prologue to the Lukan writings, which is extant only in Latin, has preserved a tradition according to which St. Luke died in Bithynia at the age of seventy-four.

During the 19th century excavations in Ephesus, J.T. Wood discovered a circular monument southwest of the Magnesia Gate. A pilaster with a relief of a cross and a bull, the symbol of St. Luke, led Mr. Wood to the incorrect conclusion that the monument was the tomb of St. Luke. The only other evidence in support of this identification was that "the Greek Archbishop of Smyrna had found it stated in a historical work in his library that St. Luke died in Ephesus." In fact, the building was a former Greek temple turned into a church during the Byzantine period.

The Legend of Abgar

In the latter part of the 19th century Austrian archaeologists discovered on the northern side of the Arcadian Way a lintel inscribed with the lengthy Greek text of the apocryphal correspondence between Jesus Christ and King Abgar of Mesopotamia. The text of the Ephesus lintel is similar to that given by the 4th century bishop Eusebius. Abgar, afflicted with a dreadful and incurable disease, sent a letter to Jesus acknowledging His divinity, requesting His help, and offering Him asylum in his own residence because of Jesus' difficulties with the Jews. "I have heard the reports respecting thee and thy cures, as performed by thee without medicines and without the use of herbs." According to the legend, Jesus wrote declining the offer, promising, however, that after He ascended He would send one of His disciples to heal the king's affliction and give life both to the king and to his family. After the ascension, Thaddaeus, one of the disciples, was sent to Edessa and delivered Abgar and his son Abdas from their sufferings. It is generally believed that these letters were written about the year 200. Pope Gelasius (492-496 A.D.) and a Roman synod (495 A.D.) rejected the correspondence as apocryphal.

The Seven Sleepers of Ephesus

The extensive Grotto of the Seven Sleepers of Ephesus, one of the popular medieval pilgrimage shrines of Eastern and Western Christians, is at the foot of Mt. Pion. The tradition of the Seven Sleepers of Ephesus states that sometime in the 3rd century seven young princes of the imperial court — Achillides, Diomedes, Diogenes, Probatus, Stephanus, Sambatius, and Cyriacus — were converted to the Christian faith and upon their baptism adopted the names Maximianus, Malchus, Martianus, Constantinus, Dionysius, John, and Serapion. During the violent persecutions of the emperor Decius (249-251 A.D.) they were ordered to publicly offer sacrifices to the idols. They refused and fled to a cave at the foot of a nearby mountain in which they fell asleep. Their malefactors closed up the cave and the seven young princes slept for almost two hundred years. During the reign of Theodosius II, in 446 A.D., the young princes awoke to find that the wall which had imprisoned them had crumbled. Malchus, one of their number, went to the nearest village to buy food. The young prince chose

The Seven Sleepers of Ephesus
Icon by Emmanuel Tzane (d. 1690)
Benaki Museum, Athens, No. 560

what he wanted but when he offered to pay with an old imperial coin the shopkeeper discovered the miracle. At this time Ephesus was a Christian city and the news of the Seven Sleepers spread rapidly until it reached the imperial court. Several bishops and the emperor himself went to Ephesus to verify the story. Before their arrival, however, the young princes died, although their bodies remained uncorrupted.

Theodosius ordered the construction of a large basilica to enshrine the youths' place of refuge. Christians also venerated the tomb of St. Mary Magdalene at the entrance of the grotto. During the Middle Ages the cult of the Seven Sleepers of Ephesus spread widely. In the 11th century their relics in the Church of Santa Maria del Popolo in Rome attracted pilgrims from all over the world, and many shrines and churches were consecrated in their honor. In the beginning of the 12th century the Russian abbot Daniel referred to the Cave of the Seven Children, leading us to assume that the cave was still intact. The large number of 14th and 15th century graffiti by Frankish, Greek, and Armenian pilgrims adorning the walls of the catacomb indicate how long it was regarded as an important center of pilgrimage. In the 17th century, Simeon of Poland described the site as being destroyed, and one hundred years later the cult seemed to have been transferred from Ephesus to the cave church of St. Solomoni and the Seven Maccabean Youths in Paphos in Cyprus. In his *Description of the East,* the 18th century traveler Richard Pococke mentioned that in Paphos there was "a church under ground cut out of the rock, dedicated to the Seven Sleepers." The Seven Maccabean Youths had changed into the Seven Sleepers of Ephesus!

The cult of the Seven Sleepers spread beyond the bounds of Christianity. In the 18th sûrah of the Koran, called "the cave," their story is told with some alterations and additions, the most obvious being the dog Qitmir, who was trapped along with the seven princes. According to Islamic tradition, their names were

Ephesus: The Church of the Seven Sleepers

Jemlika, Meshilina, Mislina, Mernûs, Debbernûs, Shazzernûz, and Kephestatjus, and these names were believed to have magical power to protect houses from being burned. The names also were engraved on bracelets as a protection against the evil eye. In the 9th century the caliph al-Wathiq obtained the special authorization of the Byzantine emperor Michael III for an Arab scholar to visit the caves in which the relics of the seven youths were believed to be preserved. The popularity of the cult of the Seven Sleepers among Muslims is seen by the numerous pilgrimage shrines in their honor, the best known being the caves of al-Kahf northwest of Tarsus, at Yarpuz near Maraš, and at Qâsiyûn northwest of Damascus.

Excavations at the Ephesian grotto were carried out from 1926 to 1928. An extensive cemetery and the remains of a church were unearthed beneath large masses of rocks and sand. Below the church the Austrian archaeologists discovered a large catacomb with ten chambers.

The Third Ecumenical Council of Ephesus

The ecumenical councils at Nicaea in 325 A.D. and Constantinople in 381 A.D. asserted the full humanity and divinity of Christ without, however, defining the manner of their union. The problem left was to solve the apparent incongruity of this union and to determine the exact mode of this coincident identity and difference. Apollinaris, by defending the unity of Christ, had tried to show that Christ the Man was the second Person of the Trinity. In doing this he substituted the divine Logos for the human spirit of Jesus, thereby detracting from the fullness of Christ's humanity. On the other hand, Nestorius, the bishop of Constantinople, destroyed the unity of Christ's person by affirming that the Logos began to dwell in a special manner in Jesus some time after His birth, which meant that it was absurd and blasphemous to call the Holy Virgin the Mother of

God. For him she was the "Mother of Christ" in whom God later came to dwell. Cyril of Alexandria, who had stated the doctrine of the perfect union of two natures in one person, opposed this view. The theological controversy was intensified by the personal rivalry between Cyril and Nestorius, both of whom claimed the primacy of the East. Nestorius began excommunicating members of his church who refused to subscribe to his teachings and, as bishop of Constantinople, sought support from the emperor Theodosius II. Cyril looked to Rome for support. On November 3, 430 A.D., Cyril called together the bishops of the East in Alexandria to examine the doctrines of Nestorius, which they found heretical. Cyril then issued the famous twelve *Anathemata*. If Nestorius did not accept the *Anathemata* he was to be deposed. Nestorius and his followers rejected the ultimatum and accused Cyril of heresy.

The need for an ecumenical council was great. Theodosius II convoked a council that was to begin on Pentecost of 431 A.D. in Ephesus. To safeguard the rights of the Bishop of Rome, Pope Celestine I sent two bishops and one priest with instructions to attach themselves firmly to Cyril of Alexandria. When the council opened most of the bishops present were from the East. Neither the papal legates nor John, the patriarch of Antioch and a supporter of Nestorius, had arrived. After sixteen days of waiting, Cyril decided to open the council on 22 June 431 A.D. Nestorius attended with six and Cyril with about fifty bishops. Memnon, the bishop of Ephesus, was present with about forty of his suffragan bishops and twelve from Pamphylia. On the opening day 159 bishops attended the council, although 198 signatures appeared on the final document. The emperor was represented by Count Candidian. Nestorius was asked three times to appear, but he refused. The letters of Cyril of Alexandria and Celestine of Rome, in which Nestorius was condemned, were read and accepted. The Council declared Nestorius deposed as bishop of Constantinople and excommunicated him for his heretical teachings. That evening the people of Ephesus celebrated this triumph with a procession carrying torches and incense in honor of the Virgin Mary, who was now officially given the title of God-Bearer.

A few days later John, patriarch of Antioch, arrived. He joined Count Candidian who assembled forty-three bishops in a rebel council which deposed Cyril and Memnon of Ephesus, and excommunicated their followers. On July 10 the papal legates finally arrived and approved the proceedings of the Council, declaring the sessions of the rebel council invalid. The final sessions were held from 10 July to 31 August, 431 A.D.

The Council convened in the Church of the Holy Virgin in the northwest section of the city. The church was built on the site of a 2nd century Roman building which has been identified with the *museion*, the high school of Ephesus, or the corn and money exchange. Those who argue for the *museion* maintain that the two exedrae in the apses at the ends of the building served as tribunals where the final examinations were held. Those who argue for the corn and money exchange point to the 2nd century rhetorician Aristeides who refers to Ephesus as the bank for the province of Asia. Perhaps customers gathered here to examine the produce on display while bankers and brokers occupied the small rooms in the aisles.

During the 4th century the building was converted into a church with three naves, the central one finishing in a semi-circular apse. The eastern section of the building was the residence for the bishop. The baptistery on the north side of the atrium was built in the 4th century. On 26 July 1967, Pope Paul VI offered supplications (preces effudit) in this sacred House of God, by his presence reaffirming the importance of this once great Christian city.

Ephesus: The Church of the Holy Virgin

Epilogue

"O how quickly passes away the glory of the earth" said Thomas à Kempis. As one walks through the ruins of this historic city, one may easily be reminded of the pronouncements of the Sibyllian Oracle, written in the 2nd century A.D., projecting the future of the city of Diana:

> Where is thy sacred fame, proud Ephesus,
> Raised to honor of Latona's child?
> Like as the ship by stormy billows riv'n,
> Sinks in the vortex of the whirling wave,
> So the bright emblem of Ionia's state
> Shall sink, confounded, in the mighty deep.

Where once men and women caught the fire of the new faith and laid the spiritual and intellectual foundations of the Christian Church, where chapels, churches, and cathedrals were erected in honor of God, here today thousands of visitors ramble through the deserted fragments of an abandoned city. The relevance of this observation cannot be exaggerated by the student of history and religion. My own feelings concur with those of Thomas Smith, British chaplain at Constantinople, who, visiting Ephesus 300 years ago, stood among the ruins, and confessed:

> That which affected me with the deepest anguish and most sorrowful resentment when I was upon the place, and does still, was and is a reflection upon the threat made against Ephesus: "Remember then from what you have fallen, repent and do the works you did first. If not, I will come to you and remove your lampstand from its place, unless you repent." As I sorrowfully walked through the ruins of that city, I concluded most agreeably that the sad and direful calamities which have involved these Asian Churches ought to proclaim to the present flourishing churches of Christendom, what they are to expect, and what may be their case one day, if they follow their evil example, that their candlestick may be removed too, except they repent,

and that their security lyes not so much in the strength of their frontiers and the greatness of their armies, for neither of these could defend the Eastern Christians from the invasion and fury of the Saracens, as in their mutual agreements and in the virtues of the Christian life.

INDEX

135

136

BIBLIOGRAPHY

Akurgal, E., *Ancient Civilizations and Ruins of Turkey*. Istanbul, 1970.

Alzinger, Wilhelm, *Die Stadt des siebten Weltwunders*. Wien, 1962.

Arundell, F.V.J., *Discoveries in Asia Minor*. 2 vols. London, 1834

Ballance, M., "The Site of Derbe: A New Inscription," *Anatolian Studies*, VII, 1957, pp. 145-151.

Bean, George E., *Turkey's Southern Shore*. London, 1968.

Bean, George E., *Turkey Beyond the Meander*. London, 1971.

Bornkamm, Günther, *Paulus*. Stuttgart, 1969.

Buckler, W.H. and Calder, W.M., *Monumenta Asiae Minoris Antiqua*, Vol. VI, *Monuments and Documents from Phrygia and Caria*. Manchester, 1939.

Cobham, Claude D., *Excerpta Cypria. Materials for a History of Cyprus*. Cambridge, 1908.

Conybeare, W.J. and Howson, J.S., *The Life and Epistles of St. Paul*. London, 1863.

Deutsch, Bernard F., *Our Lady of Ephesus*. Milwaukee, 1965.

Duncan, G.S., *St. Paul's Ephesian Ministry*. Hodder & Stoughton, 1929.

Falkener, Edward, *Ephesus and the Temple of Diana*. London, 1862.

Falkener, Edward, "Letter from Edward Falkener upon the so-called Tomb of St. Luke at Ephesus," *Transactions of the Society of Biblical Archaeology*, VII, 1882, pp. 241-247.

Fellows, Charles, *A Journal written during an Excursion in Asia Minor*. London, 1839.

Filson, Floyd V., "Ephesus and the New Testament," *Biblical Archaeologist*, VIII, 1945, pp. 73-80.

Finegan, Jack, *Light from the Ancient Past*. Volume II, Princeton U. Press, 1959.

Goodspeed, Edgar J., *An Introduction to the New Testament*. Chicago, 1937.

Gunnis, Rupert, *Historic Cyprus*. London, 1936.

Hogarth, David George, *Devia Cypria*. Oxford, 1889.

Hogarth, David George, *Excavations at Ephesus. The archaic Artemesia*. London, 1908.

James, Montague R., *The Apocryphal New Testament*. Oxford, 1926.

Johnson, Shermane, "Laodicea and its Neighbours," *Biblical Archaeologist*, XIII, 1950, pp. 1-18.

Josephus, Flavius, *Jewish Antiquities*. Books XIV & XVI.

Karageorghis, Vassos, *Salamis in Cyprus. Homeric, Hellenistic and Roman*, London, 1969.

Kiepert, Henri, *Atlas Antiquus*. Berlin, 1908.

Kleiner, Gerhard, *Das Römische Milet*. Wiesbaden, 1970.

Macgregor, G.H.C., "The Acts of the Apostles" *The Interpreter's Bible*, Vol. IX.

Mansel, Arif Müfid and Akarca, Aşkidil, *Excavations and Researches at Perga*. Ankara, 1949.

Michaelis, Wilhelm, "Das Gefängnis des Paulus in Ephesus," *Byzantinisch - Neugriechische Jahrbücher*, VI, 1927 - 1928, pp. 1 - 18.

Morton, H.V., *In the Steps of St. Paul*. London, 1963.

Murphy, John L., *The General Councils of the Church*. Milwaukee, 1960.

Ogg, George, *The Odyssey of Paul. A Chronology*. Old Tappan, N.J., 1968.

Palma di Casnola, Louis, *Cyprus: Its Ancient Cities, Tombs and Temples*. London, 1877.

Parvis, Merrill M., "Archaeology and St. Paul's Journeys in Greek Lands," Part 4, Ephesus, *Biblical Archaeologist*, VIII, 1945, pp. 62-73.

Ramsay, William Mitchell, *The Cities of St. Paul*. Longson, 1907.

Ramsay, William Mitchell, *St. Paul the Traveller and the Roman Citizen*. London, 1927.

Robinson, David M., "A Preliminary Report on the Excavations at Pisidian Antioch and at Sizma," *American Journal of Archaeology*, XXVIII, 1924, 4, pp. 435-444.

Robinson, David M., "Roman Sculptures from Colonia Caesarea (Pisidian Antioch)," *Art Bulletin,* IX, 1926-1927, pp. 5-69.

Simpson, William, "The Supposed Tomb of St. Luke at Ephesus," *Transactions of the Society of Biblical Archaeology,* VI, 1878, pp. 323-326.

Sterrett, J.R. Sitlington, "An Epigraphical Journey in Asia Minor during the summer of 1884." *Papers of the American School of Classical Studies at Athens,* Vol. II, 1883-1884.

Sterrett, J.R. Sitlington, "The Wolfe Expedition to Asia Minor." *Papers of the American School of Classical Studies at Athens,* Vol. III, 1888.

Sukenik, E., *Ancient Synagogues in Palestine and Greece.* London, 1934.

Tonneau, P.R., "Ephèse au temps de saint Paul." *Revue biblique,* XXXVIII, 1929, pp. 5-34, 320-363.

Wheler, George, *A Journey into Greece.* London, 1682.

Wood, C.T., *The Life, Letters and Religion of St Paul.* Edinburgh, 1925.

Wood, J.T., *Discoveries at Ephesus.* London, 1877.

Wood, J.T., "On the Antiquities of Ephesus having Relation to Christianity," *Transactions of the Society of Biblical Archaeology,* VI, 1878, pp. 327-333.

Zimmermann, G., *Ephesos im ersten christlichen Jahrhundert.* Leipzig, 1874.

In the Footsteps of the Saints
A new series of travel guides

Otto F.A. Meinardus

A new series of inexpensive guides for travellers and others interested in retracing the journeys of early Christian figures. The geographical context of the lands described is supplemented by historical accounts, references to recent archaeological finds and observations about the life and customs of the inhabitants.

Each title is about 160 pages and is available in either a paperback or hardback version; the text is illustrated by many photographs. All books are uniform in format, 5½" x 8¼".
PRICE: $4.95 (paperback)
$7.50 (hardcover)

ST. PAUL IN EPHESUS and the Cities of Galatia and Cyprus
ISBN 0-89241-044-2 (paperback)
0-89241-071-x (hardcover)

ST. PAUL IN GREECE
ISBN 0-89241-045-0 (paperback)
0-89241-072-8 (hardcover)

ST. PAUL'S LAST JOURNEY
ISBN 0-89241-046-9 (paperback)
0-89241-073-6 (hardcover)

ST. JOHN OF PATMOS and the Seven Churches of the Apocalypse.
ISBN 0-89241-043-4 (paperback)
0-89241-070-1 (hardcover)

CARATZAS BROTHERS, PUBLISHERS
246 Pelham Road
New Rochelle, New York 10805